The Leviathan:
The Nation Testifies

By Steve Box

No individual in this ministry will violate the confidence of any persons or organizations to incriminate, convict or aid in the area of law enforcement. We are committed to staying neutral in these situations.

All Scripture quotations are taken from the King James Version of the Bible.

Acknowledgments

This book is dedicated to the Father, Son and Holy Ghost and to every child that has lost their parents to the drug world! To the many who are taking back their lives!

Special thanks to cover artist and friend Terry Ward.

Table of Contents

Section 1

Section 2

Foreword

This morning I am sitting at my computer searching for the words that will make a difference in someone's life. What are they? What is it that I can say to you, that will make a difference? What you are about to read over these next pages are what the Holy Spirit has led me to write unto you. I believe in the times that we are living in there is a plan, a way out for every one who wants out of the world of drugs. Isaiah chapter 55 verse 9 says "For as the heavens are higher than the earth, so are my ways higher than your ways, and my thoughts than your thoughts." Isaiah chapter 55 verse 11 says "So shall my word be that goeth forth out of my mouth: it shall not return void, but it shall accomplish that which I please, and it shall prosper in the thing whereto I sent it." I believe what the Word of God says and it says that it will accomplish what it was sent to do! I believe that the Lord is sending a message from His word to you through this book. What I want to do is to prophesy life to your situation, whatever it might be. Over the past two years we have seen people reached, who many thought were unreachable, families put back together, lives restored and thousands born into the kingdom of God! The Lord is sending a message to us all, what is the drug world really? John 8:32 says "You shall know the truth and the truth will set you free." This book *The Leviathan The Nation Testifies* is making a statement to you. This statement is that God has a name for the world of drugs and it is called sorcery! The nation has testified through thousands and thousands of letters that what is contained in these pages is the truth. While this book will focus mainly on methamphetamine, all of the other man made drugs are sorcery also! So I challenge you if your drug of choice was crack, or heroin, pharmaceuticals or any other drug to put that drug name in the place of meth as you read this book. Ezekiel 37:10 says "So I prophesied as he commanded me and the breath came into them and they lived, and stood up upon their feet, an exceeding great army." Sides are being chosen, where are you? The Lord is putting together a great army for the final harvest. So today wherever you are jail, home, work or elsewhere I want to speak life, recovery, restoration, into you and your families situation, in the Name of Jesus!

The Leviathan

The Websters Dictionary calls *Leviathan* a sea monster or any huge thing. Any huge thing, methamphetamine is covering our United States as well as the world. Meth labs of every shape, size and in almost any location, are pumping out quantities of poison to kill, steal and destroy unlike anything there has ever been before in the world of drugs. I heard a quote from the drug czar that methamphetamine is the worst thing that has ever happened to America.

Ask any law enforcement agency that is waging war against meth and they'll tell you they've never seen anything like it before. Not only are there people from every walk of life cooking meth, there are also giant super labs, that are producing meth by the ton. August 1, 2000 cnn.com reports U.S. drug agents dismantle nationwide trafficking ring. Attorney General Janet Reno and DEA administrator Donnie Marshall announced that Operation Mountain Express, began in December 1999, had seized 8 million in cash, 10 metric tons of pseudoephedrine, capable of producing 18,000 lbs. of finished methamphetamine. Also seized was 83 lbs. of finished product, two pseudoephedrine extraction laboratories, one meth laboratory and 136 lbs. of processing chemicals. This is only one example of a large organization. Information from the internet says that Hawaii is being overran with meth, that is being produced in Southeast Asia, and the Philippines. If the general public only knew the atrocities that go on the world of meth, there should be a great outcry. I was recently giving a Meth Awareness seminar, with the head of the southwest Missouri Drug task force, and one of his top investigators. A question was asked about how much of the violent crime being committed in Southwest Missouri is connected with methamphetamine. Now I'm talking about murders, suicides, rapes, abductions, child molestations, stealing and thefts and so on.

The answer was almost unbelievable, He said he believed 95%! Now this would be hard for some to believe, but if you have ever been a hardcore meth addict you would say that's about right.

As I write this Meth is covering the United States like an out of control cancer, a runaway train, a blanket of sorcery unlike anything before. In the book of Job chapter 41, the entire chapter talks about the Leviathan, it's comparison with Methamphetamine is amazing. In Job 41:6 it says, "Shall the companions make a banquet of him? Shall they part him among the merchants?" (Another word for merchants is dealers.) In the book of Revelations 18:23 says, "For thy merchants were the great men of the earth; for by thy sorceries were all nations deceived."

Now going back to the book of Job 41:20, it says, "Out of his nostrils goeth smoke, as out of a seething pot or cauldron." Now I want you to think about this, a seething pot or cauldron. What does a picture of a smoking cauldron summon up? Witchcraft! How about a witch or sorcerer standing in front, stirring a bubbling smoking potion. Now we're not only talking about superlabs where this is going on, but right next door, all over the nation!

Job 41:33 says, "Upon earth there is not his like, who is made without fear. Job 41:34 says, "He beholdeth all high things; he is a king over all the children of pride." Understand in the world of meth, everyone wants to become a meth cook. This is the goal! The definition of pride is an overhigh opinion of oneself, arrogance, satisfaction in one's achievement's. I encourage you to read all of Job 41 for yourself and make a comparison with methamphetamine. Understand that leviathan is a symbolic monster, a huge thing that runs off fear. In the book of Isaiah chapter 27:1 says "In that day the Lord with his sore and great and strong sword shall punish leviathan the piercing serpent, even leviathan that crooked serpent; and he shall slay the dragon that is in the sea." So what is this saying to me, it's saying methamphetamine is not going away until the day our Lord shall put all things right. But until then it is our job to try and reveal the truth and to pull as many people out of this demonic realm as we possibly can. You see we have assurance of the victory over meth and every other satanic thing. "And I saw an angel come down from heaven, having the key of the bottomless pit and a great chain in his hand. And he laid hold on the dragon, that old serpent, which is the Devil, and Satan, and bound him a thousand years" (Revelation 20:1, 2).

The Nation Testifies

Over the past one and a half years I have received thousands of letters in response to my first book *Meth = Sorcery Know the Truth*. Most all of the stories are heartbreaking, but one thing is sure, all of the letters have similarities. Not to long ago I was preparing to preach a message at Calvary Baptist Church in Joplin, Missouri. The Holy Spirit spoke to me and said the hardest thing that you will be up against is getting the general public and the church world to understand what is actually going on in the methamphetamine and drug world. We have received so many letters that it would be impossible to single out only a few, rather what I will attempt to do is pull out the similarities, to give you an overview of what is going on with everyone who becomes addicted to Meth.

"This is the third time I am coming to you. In the mouth of two or three witnesses shall every word be established" (2 Corinthians 13:1).

"I would like to tell you thank you for telling the truth about methamphetamine and exposing Satan's greatest weapon!"

****

"You have described the tricks of Satan perfectly. And I wish more people can get your book! I can tell you have had a real experience with methamphetamine. And come out on top-or as best as possible. When you have Jesus Christ you are always on the winning side." (Amen)

****

"The drug was my god and I effected many people and destroyed most I ever came in contact with. I started using meth on the weekend and whenever I could afford a $25 1/4 gram. I got to doing more and more, it went for $25, to $50, to $100 to $150 a week to every day use. So I started to sell to people at work. But it was a big hassle to go to the supplier and wait, and not have it or just not sell to me. You know how a user hates to wait on his supply! So I got to know a manufacturer, whose name I won't give. We become buddies and He showed me how to cook. The old man was known for a few murders and had stabbed a few people. He was a little crazy and you had to be on your toes. Because he was very, very paranoid. He carried a gun and two or three knives. He to tell the truth scared me, but Satan and my lust for the drug had me! I would rather get shot or stabbed than to stop messing with the drugs."

****

"I'd spent $70,000 to $80,000 and did not have nothing to show for it. But I was on the top of the world and people were my puppets, I was my own god. Or so I thought I was in the lie and taking my orders from Satan."

****

"The chemicals started to poison me and I'd been getting chemical poisoning. That's about the time I stared to go crazy paranoid and bought guns, knives and started to make bombs. The usual things people under satans control do."

****

"I did not know it but Jesus was calling me, to his son Jesus

Christ! When I was in the county jail, I started to pray. But not really meaning it you know a jail house prayer. O' God please let me out and I'll be good. Well my lawyer got me off with just a slap on the hand. Do you know it was not the mercy of the lawyer it was Christ who had mercy on me. But I was still under the control of Satan. I got out and to make a long story short four months later, I was setting in the county jail on the charge of first degree murder. I had been involved intaking another mans life a murder for hire deal. Because the man had stolen chemicals and drugs."

****

"Satan does not want to just use you, but he wants to kill you. And everyone you come in contact with."

****

"I found out that Jesus Christ, a man who I have never met, died on a cross! And Jesus Christ loves me! Me—a low-down meth cook and murderer!"

****

"So I repented of all sorcery, magic and sin and asked Jesus to save me, to show me a better way of life. And I would follow Him! "

****

"As you know time is short and Satan is using meth to get a hold of everyone he can and kill them. PLEASE KEEP TELLING PEOPLE about the dangers of meth."

****

"Your book describes my life for the five years before coming to prison. I was using and cooking meth and I did feel the evil influences guiding me. I even talked to the demons. I knew they were there. I could sense the evil in the chemicals (especially the anhydrous) and there is a "magic" that I didn't understand in the meth process. I was fully gripped in Satan's grasp. I never compared the process to alchemy before, but that is exactly what it is. The anticipation of danger and constant fear I lived through caused me to suspect everyone, bug my phone and house, and put surveillance cameras outside my house. I picked sores upon my face and body which I am scarred from. I started seeing hidden messages in everything. I would go 20 miles out of my way just to go on a five mile trip. "I can sleep when I'm dead" was a favorite saying of mine. I would get paranoid and go to a motel to hide, but then I would spend all night trying to find the microphones. Carrying a police scanner everywhere. TV screen messages. Marilyn Manson music. I lived all that nightmare. I have been in prison for one year on a six-year sentence for meth possession. I've completed two treatment programs since being here, but still felt that something was missing in my recovery. You opened my eyes to what was missing and that was God. You have changed the way I look at meth and I thank you for that. I have spent much of this year studying the Bible for the first time in my life and I didn't quite make the connection that meth was Satan's tool until now."

****

"Ya know when I was doing meth and around the people I had known all my life that were strung out on it, I felt the way your book described it. I knew it was the devil's main number one weapon against our people. I saw how fast it spread and what destruction it was doing to 'good' people lives. I even thought it had to be some sort of germ warfare because of the enormity of its destruction. I am so glad that you found the words to describe this evil potion. I have passed

your book around here but there is only one and almost 600 women. My family and a lot of my friends out there are killing themselves as I speak to meth!"

****

"The Holy Spirit showed me that I was guilty of practicing sorcery and witchcraft by practicing the craft. I was hooked on the power, however I've been sober now for about 18 months incarcerated. In mine I could put a spirit of lasciviousness, or fear, confusion or anger depending on how I wanted to do it. I too have heard voices call my name when there is no one around. The voice was familiar, but I couldn't place it. Also me and my wife have had the same hallucinations over several hours. I have seen a demon of fear literally jump on people and on everyone it jumped on they freaked out. I have had demons behind me shooting little balls at me. They streaked through the air and when they would hit me they would ignite on fire and burn me. Also back when I was using, I would have a black cat follow me everywhere I went when I was high. The cat would run alongside me with its tail straight up in the air. Sometimes I would be walking and it would run between my legs and I would trip over it. What is weird is it was all a hallucination. There has been many nights that that cat has tripped me."

****

"The Holy Spirit showed me a body which was the body of Christ and on this body was a tumor, there was veins streaking out all over from that tumor. The meth cook is that tumor and our poison is fingering out to all parts of the body like a cancer. I was so busy taking care of the craft that that is all my world would allow."

****

16

"I mean your book is telling my past life-every word, every page. It was like reading a book about myself, well about myself and what I dragged my family through. You know I never even knew that I was working for the devil. I was trying to explain to them that even though knowing what I know, I would like to forget my past and how to cook dope but I did it so many times I could do it in my sleep. Anyway telling my story to one of the jailers one of them said I've got a book for you. I guess one of the preachers had left only one in the jailers office and returned with your book. I'm sure God sent it to me. I can tell you this, it has opened my eyes to a whole new side to me and how I was living. I've only been here for three months, but was trying to get right with God but was constantly telling myself that being thrown in jail was the worst part of getting caught, cooking dope and was telling everyone that my days of cooking dope were over, only to do things differently. You see I thought I just let too many people know my bizz and if they thought I was living for God and steadily telling them that I would never cook again, I could get out someday and get away with it, I just had to do things differently. It was truly your book that made me see I wasn't fooling no one especially God, only myself."

****

"Did I write this book? Because I could have. I am crying tears of joy because I know I am not alone. Please help me! Help me! Please! I have never read a book before all the way and I can't put yours down! I am now crying a lot. I want my family and friends and mind. I was never a bad person I just made a lot of bad decisions. My body has sores all over, my mind is not clear yet. I don't know what lays ahead of me. I am scared and happy and sad and confused. Help me please God help me! My story is the same, my address is the same almost! My age is the same and I want the outcome to be the same! Help me Please!"

****

"It's so amazing the truth about the evil and cursed dope. Your book has made me realize so many things, that were right there but I could never grasp the concept of them."

****

"I read your book "Meth = Sorcery" and it had a major effect on me. I'm 34 years old and have lived a life of drugs since I was 14. I've been through everything in your book about using meth. I didn't hit rock bottom until last year when after being up three days, I got a strange feeling I'd never had before. I was hearing evil voices laughing at me and something kept poking me with something sharp. The second day it got a lot worse. I was seeing dark figures nobody else could see. I was thinking everybody else was lying about not seeing them. The third day was the worst and best day of my life. I was in town and these dark figures were surrounding me. I took off running through town. I couldn't lose them no matter how hard I tried. I ended up at a friend's house. All of a sudden I was cold. I've never been that cold. I tried to crawl into the fireplace. My friend pulled me out and put me on the couch. Then a strange power was pulling me down to where I couldn't breath. There were two voices, one telling me to let go and the other telling me to say out loud that I believe in God. I wanted to say it but I couldn't talk. My friends told me later that I quit breathing. I came to and thought I was all right but the power hit me again and the same voices came to me but I couldn't speak. I stopped breathing again but finally came to. The third time I almost gave up because the place seemed so peaceful. The voice of God told me louder and with despair to say out loud the "I believe in God" and "I love you Lord". I thought it was over, but three hours later it was dark and time for bed. I had a cross, a Bible and a picture of Jesus. I thought, "I have faith in you and I love you." I heard grunting noises and the dark figures left. I'm sure they were real demons."

****

"There are over 1200 inmates where I am and I would say at least 75% are meth addicts. This drug has tore my life apart. My families too. I know meth is sorcery in the most evil form. The only reason I'm still alive is because I have a Christian mother who has prayed me out of death. I was driving with some guys when I thought there was a cop ahead of us. I had drugs and a gun in the car. The guy wouldn't stop so I jumped out of the car. We were going fast enough that I messed my leg up. I still have the scar. I began walking on this road when I heard dogs barking. I began hallucinating that the police dogs were chasing me. I ran and hid in a corn field. I lay looking at the sky. I thought a bright star shot towards me. But it wasn't a star. I thought it might be a UFO when I realized it was a helicopter. It hovered over me and then went back into the sky. All the stars did that. Then they started dropping flares that lit up the ground. This went on all night. I was scared to death."

****

"A couple of years ago I conned a guy into lending me his truck. I told him I would be gone an hour, when I knew I would be gone for days. I promised to bring him back some dope so he agreed. The next day I was at the dope house and let someone borrow the truck. They never brought it back. After a few days, the truck owner tracked me down and kidnapped me. They took me to a house where I was beat repeatedly. They cut my shoes off with a knife and took my clothes from me. They were afraid I would try to escape. I don't know if I was hallucinating or not but I thought I heard them talk of killing me. They would beat me unconscious and then they would smoke some more meth and then they would beat on me some more."

****

"They need to hear this. They need to hear there's other people who have been through the evilness of the meth scene and found a way out through Jesus Christ."

19

****

"I was brought up in a Christian home. I left early and due to circumstances, I turned my back in anger against God. In the absence, I became involved in occult practices. All sorts, I need not bring them up here. Everything you write about and more was a part of my life. Only I had the vultures that usually accompany a funeral. I was mentally OUT THERE. I had a contact that would front me a 1/4 pound at a time. And I had all these people coming over saying they were my deceased husbands good, good friend. In that three weeks I sat in my house and watched my entire life get looted away. Someone broke into my safe and took all the titles to our vehicles and RV's. I didn't know about it right away until people started showing up wanting the vehicles. Thank you, Mr. Box for writing this book. Thank you for exposing dope for what it is-a tool of Satan. I took your book to my Bible study group tonight. These people are primarily older folks from the community who volunteer their time for us. I held up your book and said, "If you ever wanted to know what makes a meth addict tick—here it is."

****

"Needless to say Satan and his legion were alive and well within me and the torment you talked of well those things were so hideous to me that I kept them all inside where they naturally grew and manifested. Messages on my skin (backwards), the pornographic shows on static screens starring all my best friends and my ole lady, ESP, remote viewing out of body experiences, even signs of abduction by aliens, such as marks on my body as well as mental conversations have led me to the care unit. I was recommended to go to the mental hospital where I was in fact diagnosed a paranoid schizophrenic and manic depressive. I can't really go into my mind condition for fear of repercussions that it may bring upon me, but I'm sure you have an idea of what it is like with murmurs and shadows and all those other

things. I'd like to thank you for being chosen to write the book you did so that I know it is all for real, all of it! And perhaps I'm not totally insane as I have thought. Trying fruitlessly to endure all the demons and sit as though nothing was that weird."

****

"I knew that he bragged all the time about casting spells on his dope to everyone and was also perverted in all ways."

****

"My drug of choice is crack-cocaine and I have had some of the same experiences with seeing and hearing things causing me to think I was going crazy. I now understand and believe that I was being attacked by evil spirits."

****

"When I was using meth heavily, I thought I was losing my mind, my house was haunted and I was demon possessed. I called churches, talked to friends, but no one knew what was wrong. They even thought I was going crazy or hallucinating from the drugs. I was scared to death. I heard demonic voices speaking to me. I saw things that people would never believe. I had hardwood floors in my house and on two occasions I would see snakes, demons and fire in the floor. Sometimes the floor would get so hot I couldn't walk on it in my bare feet. A friend of mind was living with me and saw the same things I did. I also was afraid to take a bath because every time I did, I would see snakes swimming in the water around me. I could actually hear them hissing. I had to take quick showers. I was falling apart mentally because I didn't know what was happening to me. I thought I was going to die soon and go to hell. My friend and I got into an argument. She moved out and I experienced it all alone. I even thought of *checking into a mental hospital but my paranoid mind wouldn't let me. I kept telling myself that everyone was out to get me. If I went to the hospital they would kill me or the feds would be called and I would go to jail. I couldn't even listen to the radio. The voices and the shadows haunted me everywhere I went. I couldn't even carry on a conversation without hearing those voices."*

****

"There had been many of times when she was "coming down" after she had slept, I would find her asleep and beside her would be God's word, a Bible. I know she was looking to God for the answers."

****

"When I lived in California I lived in the high desert country for quite a while there was much satanic cult activity taking place there. Do you know of the demon pazuzu? One houseful of them had a huge statue of the demon in their yard. They held satanic rituals at night around that damnable statue. They manufactured meth and reportedly they dripped blood into the meth. Supposedly the best meth they made had baby's blood in it."

****

"I was driving a truck and got home early one day. My wife and I immediately started looking for a shot of dope. We ran into a friend of hers that had some cocaine; but I wanted to hold out for the crank. After several stops, we came home dry. I sent my wife to her friend's house for a half gram of the coke. When she got back, I took the coke to the bedroom where the equipment was. On the way past the bathroom, I grabbed some water. When I got the bag open, I poured my half plus half of my wife's in the spoon and hurry and added water in case she came into the room so she wouldn't know I was cheating. (I

got greedy) She came in just about the time I was getting ready to shoot. I was sitting at the end of the bed on a stool and she sat on the end of the bed in front of me. I found my easy spot and did it. Almost immediately my brain started screaming, "You did too much, you're dying." I stood straight up. My arms, my legs, and my whole body jerked as I fell over on the bed. I barely got, "I got it!" out of my mouth.

We lived in a 12'x60' mobile home. Our room was small. There was enough room for our double bed and our 1 year-old son's crib and a dresser. It was close quarters.

As I fell on the bed, I remember thinking, "I'll hang onto the bars of the crib." I could keep from dying. The next thing I know, I could somehow see my wife straddling me but at the same time I could see I was in a circular hollowed out place in the ground. I don't know; but in the middle of this place, I'm on a dirt stump alter and some kind of monster demon was against the wall on each side of this room. They were taking turns sending a lion out to get me. When they sent him out after me, I said an echo voice, "Get away, get away, get away." My wife thought I was talking to her. I grabbed her and in the same echoing voice I said, "Not you, not you, not you." I was aware of her presence up to this point. I will never forget the fear that consumed me. It was a shameful fear. I can't explain how frightened I was. Then all of a sudden, four little black formless creatures came and grabbed hold of my arms and legs and were dragging me down a steep coal black cliff. Automatically I was informed without me opening my mouth. I couldn't and didn't have to ask them why or where they were taking me. I already knew. I couldn't make any excuses. I couldn't even fight back. I was so scared. I knew there was no use. I was going to hell and it was too late. I couldn't stop it. Just when I had given up, God in His mercy, one more time saved me from eternal death. I didn't see Him but I know he was there for me.

"Whither shall I got from thy spirit? or whither shall I flee from thy presence? If I ascend up into heaven, thou art there: if I make my bed in hell, behold, thou art there. If I take the wings of the morning, and dwell in the uttermost parts of the sea; Even there shall thy hand

23

lead me and thy right hand shall hold me. (Psalms 139:7-10)."

****

These are not even a fraction of the testimonies and they are all the same, methamphetamine, and the drug world are sorcery in its highest degree! Make no bones about it, if you stay involved with meth you are serving the devil and his demons. There is no denying! Acts 13:10 Paul with the Holy Ghost said to the sorcerer O full of all subtilty and all mischief, thou child of the devil, thou enemy of all righteousness, wilt thou not cease to pervert the right ways of the Lord!

I like to think now of meth as the devil's seed, think about that one the next time he tempts you to ingest some of that!

Thou child of the devil is what the Word says! and I know what the devil and satan will inherit, the lake of fire! On the other hand, I have a blessed hope, and assurance, an advocate, a Father, a friend that sticks closer than a brother, someone who will never leave me nor forsake me! Praise the Lord! His name is Jesus and He's calling you!

My Story

I can remember clearly in my mind being about 7 or 8 years old and riding a church bus down to Central Assembly in Joplin and sitting in a classroom where I accepted the Lord Jesus as my Savior. After this I never really heard about God or Jesus until much later in life.

The first time I ever got drunk was at age 13. My brother who was 16 or 17 at the time took me along with some of his buddies to Kansas City, Missouri. We told our parents we were staying all night at a friend's house. On the way there I drank about nine beers and a bottle of grape wine within about 60 miles. I can remember standing on the side of the road hurling my guts out. After arriving in Kansas City, I was left in a motel room while the others went out partying. After getting so sick this cured me for a while from drinking.

At the age of 14 I had started going out with a girl that I really liked. One night we were sitting outside her house when her friend pulled up. She was a year or two older than I was. The friend asked if we wanted to smoke a joint. She said yes and I said I didn't do that. They both looked at me like I was crazy. Not too many days later she broke up with me because I didn't get high.

When I was 16 my friend who smoked pot regularly talked me into buying a bag of weed. The first three or four times I smoked it nothing happened. I had just got my drivers license. I was sitting in a drive-in movie with a girlfriend and we were smoking a joint and bam it hit me. When I closed my eyes I felt like I was flipping over backwards and then a warm pleasant feeling. After that, I was stoned and hooked. That was the summer of 1983.

I had previously broken up with my girlfriend who was to become my wife. She became pregnant and at the age of 16 in November we got married. I was trying to do the right thing. Before I go further, let me back up a little. My freshman year I had started playing football and really like it. That year I just played freshman ball then my sophomore year I started on varsity at offensive tackle. That year we made it to the semi-finals of state. The name of our school was Parkwood and had a strong football heritage with state championship teams in the past. We also had a head coach named Dewey Combs who knew how to motivate players into wanting to really destroy someone.

Then came my junior year of football. I was playing offensive guard and defensive end. Things were going great in terms of football but I was also smoking pot everyday of the week. Late in the season I got married to my first wife. After many road games we'd stop to eat and I'd sneak around the corner and get high. Only one or two guys on the team knew about this and didn't care because they usually joined me. At the end of the season we ended up 14 and 0 as the Missouri State Football Champions. We played at Busch Stadium. That year I was All Conference 1st Team, All District 1st Team, All State 1st Team and received Honorable Mention All American. After this season I started receiving a few letters from different colleges and was excited about next year's season.

On June 2, 1984 my first son, Stephen Ray Box Jr., was born. That night while my wife was in the hospital after the baby was born I left. That was the first night I became exposed to cocaine. I was 17 and I liked it.

As I started my senior year of football I was still smoking lots of pot using cocaine and drinking quite a bit. You're probably thinking, "Where were this guy's parents?" I have awesome parents. I wasn't living at home after we were married so it was easy to keep all of this hidden from them. Financially they supported my wife and I through high school. I would not be here today if it weren't for them. I mean that in more than one way.

We had a good year in football. We lost a couple of games but still ended up again in the State Championship Game at Arrowhead Stadium. However, we lost. After the season I was again All Conference, All District and All State 1st Team but this year I also received All American 1st Team honors and Blue Chip honors and was listed in the Sporting News Top 100 Recruits Nationwide. I was recruited heavily by dozens of major colleges offering full scholarships. This was 1985 and I had narrowed my choices down to The Universities of Nebraska, Arkansas, Oklahoma State and Missouri.

At this time my family and I didn't really know about Jesus. I remember Coach Fred Hatfield from Arkansas came to my parents house talking to us about going to school. He noticed a big family Bible sitting on an end table. He started talking about religion and Christ. After he left we had a little laugh and said he must have seen the Bible. At that time we didn't know the truth.

I was allowed three recruiting trips and I took them at Nebraska, OSU and MU. After visiting Nebraska and getting around Tom Osbourne, I knew that was where I wanted to go and made a verbal commitment to them. After returning my head coach didn't like the idea and said I should check out OSU and MU. I took my last trip to the University of Missouri which at the time was trying to rebuild with Coach Woody Widenhoffer. I ended up going out both nights. I went to the bars and really partied it up with some of the players. I ended up making my college decision based on the good time I had. All this time I was still smoking pot, using some cocaine and had started taking pills when I could get my hands on them.

About three weeks before I reported I stopped all drug use because I knew there would be drug tests. I finished two days and went from sixth team center to second team. School started and the first day I couldn't find my classes and decided that I didn't want to play ball after all and just left without telling anyone. That same day the guy who was first team broke his leg so I would have been starting as a freshman. After one day they realized I wasn't around and had left. Members of the coaching staff left and flew down to Joplin to try and get me to return. I didn't because what I really wanted to do was smoke pot and party.

The reason I went into this whole story about football was to show how marijuana and other drugs cost me a football career and a college education. After this I fell into a routine of working in the family business. In November 1986 I had my second son, Corey Lee Box. Now with two children, life was going along. I was smoking pot daily, hitting the alcohol and cocaine on weekends along with Zanax or Valium or painkillers, anything I could get my hands on. I was still working out on a regular basis and had also gotten into steroids both oral and injectable.

In January my best friend Randy Darby had brought a guy over to work out. He started sharing with me about Jesus and ministering to us. I accepted Jesus as my personal Savior again.

On January 20, 1987 a friend when I had just finished a workout and my wife reminded me I had to run an errand. I hadn't been doing any drugs or drinking this day. My friend, my son, Steve Jr., and I hopped in my truck and headed out. It was dark and the side roads were ice covered. We were driving out in the country to take some dog food to my in-laws.

We delivered the dog food and started back home. We were out on a dark country road with no streetlights and we were talking. I was keeping an eye out for the reflection of the stop sign, which I knew was ahead. Then out of nowhere I realized we were coming up on the intersection but there had been no sign so I slammed on the brakes and slid into the intersection. I saw the lights of an oncoming vehicle coming at us really fast. I stomped on the gas but we just sat there in the middle of the intersection, tires spinning. The vehicle hit us. I've never heard such a loud noise in my life. I woke up outside the truck lying backwards over a barbwire fence. My chest was hurting but other than that I seemed fine.

Immediately I ran to the truck to look for my son. We had been hit really hard and had rolled several times. I looked inside. He wasn't there and neither was my friend. I could hear my friend moaning. I saw that it was an ambulance that had hit us and both people in it were screaming in agony. I started searching through the snow-covered field for my boy. At this time he was only about 2 1/2 years old. I searched frantically. Finally I found him. His body was lifeless. I picked him up and wrapped him in my shirt. I ran over to the intersection and tried to flag down several cars but no one would stop.

There was a house across the road so I ran over to it and started beating on the door. No one answered. I laid my son down and tore 3 doors off their hinges to get inside. I picked him back up, took him inside and called 911. Well about this time a couple showed up who had pulled up on the accident. She immediately started administering CPR to Stevie. Another ambulance showed up from the same district that had hit us. They came in to check for a pulse and then left and went to take care of their own people. Several minutes went by before another ambulance showed up. Immediately they started pumping drugs into him, loaded him up and headed for the hospital. The whole time inside the house I'm crying out to God to help me, for this not to be happening. But my son was dead.

We left the hospital that night and the whole thing seemed like a dream—a very bad dream. Later that night I couldn't breathe right so they took me to another hospital where it was discovered that my lung had collapsed. I was admitted and wasn't able to attend Stevie's funeral. They had a service in the chapel at the hospital and brought his body up there so I could see him before they buried him. After a week or so I was released. My wife cried herself to sleep for months. She was unable to return to our house so we sold it and moved in with my parents for awhile.

After this, my entire family—parents, brother, my wife and I started attending church and were all saved. Praise God! We attended for a few months but I was soon sneaking off, smoking dope again and using steroids. After a while we built a house of our own and life fell back into the routine of work. I was also getting high morning, noon and night. I used cocaine on weekends and some during the week. I started growing my own weed and had set up a grow room in my basement. I soon moved it outside because it was a very high quality-green sinsimillia. So I became addicted to not only smoking weed but also growing it. There was also a period of using a drug called ecstasy which is a derivative of methamphetamine.

So for the next five or six years, my life revolved around whatever I could get my hands on—mostly pills, cocaine and acid. During this time I also had two knee operations which just boosted my addiction for painkillers.

I became involved in martial arts and received my black belt in Mong Su Don Tai, which is a Chinese soft style. The meaning is the "instinctive prowess of a wild beast." So my life revolved around work, karate and drugs.

During this time I had two more wonderful children, Jeremiah Andrew Box, born July 23, 1991 and Katie Madison Box, born July 1, 1993. Back in 1988 I had wanted to open a gym. I had some equipment, but needed more. Instead of buying it I bought a welder, a chop saw and other tools and a friend taught me how to weld. So we built the equipment needed. The gym went out of business but I started building weight equipment for area high schools and individuals. I became very successful and soon had a brochure that I distributed and was receiving orders from all over. I built mostly for high schools but I also built complete gyms and delivered them to New Orleans, Maine, Kentucky, etc.

Once the equipment was built I also delivered it. During the period of time after my son's death there was a wedge of unforgiveness and blame driven between my wife and myself. She blamed me for our son's death and I blamed myself. As I delivered this weight equipment, I stopped in a bar and met a girl. I ended up pursuing this woman and started an affair that lasted about seven months. I was sneaking around behind my wife's back. This girl was also living with someone and had to sneak around also. After seven months I came home one day and told my wife it was over—I was leaving. At this time I left my wife and three children. We had been married ten years and, at the drop of a hat, I destroyed our marriage.

I couldn't live without this other woman any longer. After I left my wife I helped my girlfriend move out while her boyfriend was at work. We rented a small house and moved in together. This was January 1994. From this point on and for the next four years is somewhat of a methamphetamine nightmare.

During the first part of 1994 my divorce proceedings got started. After my girlfriend and I moved in together we started a regular regiment of partying. During this time I was still building some weight equipment. We were drinking heavy and beginning to use meth. I had used meth a few times in previous years but always preferred cocaine then.

I remember one night we had been drinking heavily, popping pills and up on crystal meth. We were sitting on the couch in the living room when all of a sudden my hands and arms locked up and curled up into a twisted fashion. Then my entire body began convulsing uncontrollably, jerking in an almost rhythmic fashion. Daella, my girlfriend began crying and was asking me what she should do. I didn't know what to do. I had no control over the limbs of my body. They just kept jerking uncontrollably. All I could tell her was as long as this action didn't move to my heart that it would be okay. This went on for a couple of hours. Eventually it died down and went away. The next few days my motor skills didn't function quite right but they soon returned. You'd think that would have cured me from wanting more drugs but within a few hours I was on my way to get more crystal.

Over the next set of months our use of meth was gradually increasing. I also need to point out that the rebellion inside of me was gradually growing. For the first time I was free to do whatever I wanted with no one to answer to and no one could tell me what to do. As the months went by violence began to creep into our relationship. At first it was mental abuse. But gradually shoving and holding down occurred while threatening break-ups, which every few months were taking place. I thought I wanted to be completely free to do whatever I pleased. This went on and off during most of 1994. The enemy was laying the mental scars.

Towards the end of 1994 we were together again and started using meth on a daily basis. The supply was flowing on a regular basis by now from several directions. The days turned into weeks on end with no sleep. The audio and visual hallucinations were beginning to set patterns in the direction that Meth would take us.

In January 1995 I had been awake for 19 days with no sleep. My girlfriend had dropped out and slept after 15 days. I finally slept one night then started all over again. I don't know exactly how to explain being ganked on meth for long periods of time except that your grip on reality disappears. You enter a world where all that matters is more and more meth and whatever you are hallucinating at any given moment. During these times I didn't realize the connection between meth and sorcery. At first I thought it was the greatest thing there was.

Around February I got a new connection out of Tulsa, Oklahoma where the supply was plentiful of all types of drugs. I became more and more strung out. I was carrying at least one 357 magnum at all times if not two and also a couple of fighting knives. I thought I was invincible. The meth was driving this at all times. I would prepare myself mentally to do whatever was necessary in case a deal went wrong. This period of time is a blur except I know I hardly ever bathed and thrived on the grunge that went along with meth.

For several months I slept only a few hours every few weeks. I started getting a cough that grew progressively worse. During this time there was always a group of guys hanging out and I still had one friend that was working for me whom I trusted. Most of the time we would have a bonfire going next to my metal shop for weeks.

Around April I developed walking pneumonia and didn't know it. I had a five gallon bucket of marijuana, a small tackle box full of Valium, Zanax, Mexican Quaaludes, Halcyons and some other downers, sheets of blotter acid, crank or meth, cocaine and some heroin. I had been consuming all of this with large quantities of beer for several weeks. Finally it caught up with me. I found myself lying in bed unable to even sit up. My parents showed up and called an ambulance. The police showed up also. All I could tell my dad was not to let them in the house. At the time he met them at the door as they were taking me out on a stretcher to the ambulance. Somehow, thank God, they didn't go in. I had always told Daella if the cops ever came, to flush everything she could and my friend who I trusted knew where I kept the stash in the shop. I told him if the cops ever showed up to pitch it in the fire if we had one going, which we did at the time.

I was lying in the hospital coughing up blood and I remember my dad asking the doctor how I was. He said that if I made it through the night I would be okay. I made it through the night and after a day or so Daella and my buddy showed up at the hospital. She told me she had flushed the pills and everything else. I went ballistic, even though she just did what I had told her to do. I jumped up and ripped the IV's out of my arms and wanted to strangle her. My friend had told Daella and others that he had thrown the marijuana in the fire. But in the hospital he told me he had hid it in a brush pile in the woods. That was the only thing that kept me from losing it because we were talking about thousands of dollars flushed down the toilet.

I checked myself out of the hospital and rested a few days but started right back in. I didn't drink for a few weeks in order to let the antibiotics build up my system. But everything else was going full blast, mostly meth and marijuana.

I was in constant torment over the drugs being flushed. It drove me insane and I was always abusing Daella mentally. By the end of May 1995 my suppliers had dried up. One guy had shot himself and another was just out after he lost his supplier. There were small quantities around but I couldn't get my hands on larger quantities.

One day I saw a friend that told me he had a connection in Fontana, California. This is a suburb about 30 miles from LA. I told him if he would hook me up I'd take him to do a deal. He introduced us and we struck up a bargain on what would be his end. Within a few days, Daella, this guy and myself headed for LA. It took a couple of days to get to Laughlin, Nevada where I got Daella a room and then we headed over to Fontana to try and set up this deal. At first the guy involved freaked out that he had brought a stranger to his house but within a few hours I convinced them I was no cop. That night we scored some crystal to get us by until he could nail down a pound the next day. We returned to Laughlin and waited for several hours. He called back and it was set. We returned and made the deal. The guy I took out there got part of the dope I owed him and then wanted to borrow my Jeep which I said was no problem but to be back in a few hours so we could leave.

Pure meth distorts time and reality. Before I knew it, it was the next day. I was in Fontana and had bought an old 1969 Nova that I decided to tow back. It was insane but at the time it seemed like what I wanted. The next few days became a blur as I forgot about Daella in Laughlin. I forgot that I was from Missouri and fell into something like a trance. I took on a Mexican accent and thought these guys were my brothers. We went to the salvage yard, pulled parts and an engine. A couple of days went by as we partied. The guy I took out there was always going partying with other friends he knew there. After a couple of days it hit me. Daella was in Laughlin. I was surrounded by a group of individuals I didn't know and was carrying a pound of pure.

I began to feel my life could be in jeopardy. Although I was armed and prepared mentally I knew I needed to leave. It was around noon one day when I told the guy who was with me to be back by dark and we would leave. Well nighttime came and this guy was late. Finally he showed up and I lost it. I told him to get his bag and hit the road, that he wasn't going back with me. About this time a couple of guys wanted to borrow my Jeep to take a girl home. So I let them. They returned with this story how four car loads of cops had pulled them over and searched the Jeep. Whether this was true I didn't know because the guy I told to hit the road could have turned me in.

We hooked up the Nova to my jeep. I was trying to decide how I could leave. If what they said was true then the cops could have been waiting for me to leave. I called my karate instructor back home and asked him how I should get out of there. By this time there were several people doing meth in the garage. People were coming and going, buying dope. I worked out a deal for them to drive my Jeep to Laughlin the next day. I waited for one of the guys there to leave and I got in the car with him. I had my pound of meth that I was willing to do anything for at the time.

I had him drop me off at the airport in Ontario CA, which is near Fontana. It was the middle of the night and no car rentals were open. I was trying to keep my mind together, fighting the hallucinations. I got into a taxi. He said "Where to?" I said "I don't know. The next town I guess." So we drove a while and I told him I needed to get to Laughlin, Nevada. He pulled over and called his dispatcher and got a price of $480 to take me there. By this time I was running low on cash but luckily I still had my credit cards. So I basically took a three or four hour, $500 taxi ride back to Laughlin.

I was relieved to be back where Daella was but I was still tweaked out of my head. I figured by this time the guy I had left in Fontana had possibly tipped off the law back home. I was doing more and more dope, not wanting to come down which was a big mistake. I called the guy that had been my supplier in Tulsa and he agreed to fly to Las Vegas and help me transport the pound back.

Daella and I rented a car in Laughlin and drove to Las Vegas. I called the guys back in Fontana who had my Jeep and Nova. I arranged for them to drive it to Las Vegas, meet me and buy bus tickets to send them back. So Daella and I arrived in Las Vegas later that day and met the guy from Tulsa in a low rent sleazy motel room. We started trying to hatch out

35

a deal we could both be happy with. That night turned completely bad. I tweaked out on him, became paranoid that he was possibly a cop and by no means was there going to be any kind of deal reached. I unloaded my guns just in case he was a cop and denied they were mine which was ludicrous. Early in the night we had packaged the meth in cellophane in the shape of a snake so that it could be worn around the neck, under a jacket.

It was getting so bizarre in that motel room that I went to get some air. I took the dope with me and threw it on top of a restaurant across the street. I went back to the motel room and this guy freaked because the dope was gone. I told him it was in a safe place. After an hour we talked it over and he agreed to fly the dope back and we would work out a deal back in Tulsa. We walked across the street and I climbed up the building, got the dope and came back down. I had also hid my personal stash in the paper towel dispenser in the restaurant's bathroom.

The meth took over again and the paranoia got to the point I was contemplating how I could kill this guy and get out of there. I looked out the window and saw swat teams on top of the building. I know now it was an hallucination. He must have sensed this while I went into the bathroom. He told Daella he was leaving for a little bit because he thought I was going to kill him.

I woke Daella up. She had been trying to sleep during all of this. She was pregnant at the time. The sun was beginning to come up so we got our things together, got in the rental car and drove to a pay phone. I called my dad. We had been gone about 10 or 12 days. Daella had spoken with one of her friends back home who relayed what was happening to my parents. My dad said, "Don't worry about what's happened just get rid of what you got, and come home." I got out of the car and told Daella to drive to the airport to the American Airlines counter and I would meet her there. I took off across a construction site on foot and Daella headed to the airport. I wanted to stash the dope until I could figure out what was really going on. I started running across this site when a couple of guys started yelling at me to stop and they started chasing me. Now I don't know whether they were real or hallucinations. There was no way to tell. I was running in 100-degree weather with jeans, a long sleeve shirt and a jean jacket on. Sweating profusely, my heart was about to pump out of my chest.

I came to a hedge about six feet tall that ran alongside a highway. I tried to dive through it but it stuck me in mid-air. I pulled my self through and started looking for a place to stash the dope. There was some kind of metal box sticking out of the ground so I dug a hole in the sand and buried the Meth. I jumped up still running because I felt like I was being pursued. I ran across the highway into one of the casinos. I tried to slow down and walk. I got to a phone but I don't know who I called. Maybe I didn't call anyone. But I could see that the casino security had picked up on me so I ran out of the casino into another. I threw the knives I was carrying on top of a cabinet. I had left my pistols in the car with Daella.

At the next casino I ended up running out a back entrance and a man in a small black sports car stopped. I told him I was trying to get to the airport and he gave me a ride. I found Daella and we got another motel room. While all this was going on the guys from Fontana had driven my Jeep and Nova up to Las Vegas. We were to meet at McDonalds. Our wires got crossed between two different McDonalds so they waited a long time then headed back to Fontana. They later said the Jeep was overheating so they left the Nova in a parking lot next to McDonalds and drove the Jeep back to Fontana. I was able to contact them later by phone. They told me what had happened and where the Nova was so I said I'd be down in the morning to pick up my Jeep. I did get some sleep that night.

The next morning we drove back, dropped the car at the rental agency and got the Jeep. Since I had stashed all my dope in the sand I got about one gram to hold me over. The plan was to drive back to Las Vegas, retrieve the dope from where I hid it, pick up the Nova and head home. We drove back to Las Vegas. I had been doing a lot of meth with these guys before we left and was beginning to hallucinate pretty hard about the time we hit the Las Vegas city limits. To me it looked like a cop was getting ready to pull us over so I ate about 1 gram of meth. I knew after I ate it, it was too much. We tried to find a hotel to check into and ended up at the Luxor Hotel, the big pyramid shaped hotel. We checked in but I was already beginning to tweak out. I tried to hold it together. It seemed like an eternity to get our keys and in my paranoid mind they were stalling in order to bug our room.

Finally we got the keys. We got in the room. Daella was trying to sleep while I began looking around for anything suspicious. The voices in my head began to intensify their attack. They said, "That guy from Tulsa is here with some of his buddies now and they've got your room bugged to the gills. They are waiting for the perfect time to get you." Then it changed. The voices told me there were cops, Daella was helping them and they've stashed a large amount of meth. You are going to get busted regardless.

I started dismantling the room. One of the first things I did was look under the smoke alarm. When I undid this it must have sent a signal because a maintenance guy showed up to check. I told him I was just curious and that I had hooked it back up. He left but must have seen the condition I was in and called security. Things proceeded to get worse. I barricaded a mattress set in front of the door and proceeded to dismantle the room. At the same time I could see Daella talking to someone like she was whispering into some microphone or bug maybe. I ended up in the bathroom looking frantically for the imaginary dope that I thought was hidden somewhere in the room so I could flush it. The race against time intensified.

While I was searching with my left hand I had cocked my Smith and Wesson 357 snubnose in my right. I reached down to pull the pipes under the sink when the gun went off pointed out into the hallway. I had no idea there were five or six hotel security guards on the other side of the wall. There was a pause in time. Daella ran into the bathroom. I doubled over and pretended I shot myself. Then I looked up, smiled and laughed. She ran back into the room. I heard a crash. They were breaking in the door. I tried to push against the mattress but there was too many of them. I went down to the floor as five cocked guns were at the back of my head.

Everyone's adrenaline was going crazy. I just said, "Don't shoot me, don't shoot me," pleading for my life. Thank God they didn't kill me right then and there. They handcuffed me and dragged me through the casino that been had evacuated, into a holding room where they strapped me to a bench. I was already a paranoid wreck.

I was being told they were going to shoot me up with dope and dump me in the desert. No one got away with shooting a gun in their casino. I remember other things being said but I won't go into them because I'm not sure if I was hallucinating or not.

Eventually a Clark County deputy showed up. They brought Daella down to the room I was in. I released money to her and told her to call my parents. I was building into a paranoid frenzy trying to break my handcuffs. The deputy called for another deputy to ride with us. They loaded me up and we headed toward the jail.

At that time I didn't know the Clark County jail was in downtown Las Vegas. The voices in my head were telling me they were going to kill me. They turned into an alley and I thought that was it for me. We pulled up and they got me out. They ran me into the building, trying to turn the cuffs over to take me down but I wouldn't go down. Another cop or two joined in and ran me into an elevator and bashed my head into the front of it. The fight was on. I threw two rear kicks. One connected. They spun me around and palm healed me under the nose several times. Then we all went to the floor. The elevator door opened. There were others waiting. They dragged me out and proceeded to beat me. After this they took all my clothes off and threw me into a cell. I soon realized I was on the floor. From this point hours and hours of mental abuse and mental torture proceeded.

As soon as I hit the floor I was calling out to Jesus, weeping, praying, singing. I know without a doubt it was He that spared my life several times within this one trip from Hell. The guards proceeded talk about how they were going to kill me. They would make sounds of cocking and loading guns. This went on for hours. It drove me close to insanity because I was still high on meth. After awhile I started coming down and could see it was just a game to them to torture me. This torture was one of the things that eventually helped to get me off. When I was brought in they wrote on my paperwork, "attempted murder, no bail." Within 24 hours my parents were there. They went to the Luxor, paid for the damage to the room and started looking for a lawyer. I know God somehow directed this also. They ended up with the ex-prosecuting attorney.

By now I had come down and had apologized to some of the officers. Some accepted, some didn't and I could tell they wanted to get me. The first time they shackled me and took me down to the judge they said I was still being combative. I had two evaluations by the jailhouse shrink. I told him I was on vacation, I had a drug problem and just got paranoid. I didn't mention anything else. They took me in front of the judge again. Prior to this I told my attorney about the mental torture. My mother heard him relay this information to the prosecutor. That helped plus the Luxor agreed to drop charges. I was released within about 72 hours. Before I was released I was put into a holding cell with about 30 other guys. I had the privilege of sharing about Jesus with a man there and he accepted the Lord.

Within 30 days I was back on meth and had purchased a plane ticket back to Las Vegas where I tried to retrieve that pound of meth. However I couldn't find it. I was very bitter over this entire ordeal. My pride drove me that I had been unable to return safely with these drugs. It haunted me all the time and consumed my thoughts entirely.

On July 29, 1995 Daella and I were married. I continued using heavily. In September I convinced her to fly back to Fontana with me to try and make another score. Upon arriving, I rented a car and left her in a hotel room about ten miles from where I was going. I was able to find the guys I dealt with before and everything was still cool. I wasn't able to make a deal on any quantity of meth so I scored a few pounds of marijuana and we flew back with that instead. Over the next 12 months I began on an even more downward spiral than before. Daella gave birth to our first daughter, Hailey on January 3, 1996. I continued being controlled and consumed by everything that had to do with meth.

As time passed, things became more violent. It's hard to relay exactly what goes on when you're sold out to methamphetamine. My family came in second. I got to spend the night in the county jail due to domestic violence. The spring and summer of 1996 progressively grew darker. My choice of company that summer made things worse.

An evil occurs when you combine people that have similar character-istics that feed off each other and ushers in the demonic realm. It was during this time that I witnessed along with another individual a manifesta-tion in the demonic realm. When one person is hallucinating it's easy to say they're just tweaking. It's a whole different ball game when two people are witnessing the same thing. It is completely demonic and something you'll never forget. During this year I was driving my family into financial ruin. I was only working every once in a while. We were living off of my credit cards and I was selling off my welding equipment. It was all going for more and more dope.

I had become so paranoid, and was using meth at an alarming rate. By August 1996 Daella had left me again. My dad called the sheriffs department. They showed up and loaded me up for 72 hour insanity watch. They agreed not to take me to jail if I would go to rehab so I agreed. At the rehab center everyone was talking to the doctor and no one was looking at me. I walked out, ran into the woods and got away. I called some people I knew from a convenience store. They came and picked me up. I partied with them for a day or two. That night I was coming down pretty hard and needed some more dope. One guy had some, decided he wanted to control me from getting anymore, so I left on foot. I walked about 5 miles to the north side of Joplin. I guess I passed out on the sidewalk because I woke up in the city jail. My dad and brother came down and signed for me the next morning.

I knew I wanted to quit but I didn't know the truth then. My parents took me, Daella and Hailey away for 30 days trying to help me. We got back and I stayed off meth for about 100 days but I was still smoking weed and drinking. During this entire time my mind was consumed with meth. I had acquired a book on meth manufacturing. I began acquiring everything I would need to set up my own lab so I wouldn't have to rely on anyone else for dope. One thing that drives addicts crazy is someone else having control over the dope.

By December 1996 I had acquired everything for a complete anhydrous lab. Daella and I were living in a three story duplex. It was January and I found a barn where I could try my hand at cooking dope. I had everything set and went through the entire procedure. I took my container of mineral spirits and gassed it but nothing would appear. I tried this entire procedure again and got the same results. It didn't turn out at all. I realized I wasn't getting my ephedrine separated right. In the mean time I boxed everything up and started feeling around for someone to show me exactly this step of the procedure.

By this time we had to sell our house, my new truck got repossessed and we were living in a rental property that my parents owned. We had taken the money from the house and paid off the credit cards which was a mistake. It just gave us about $60,000 worth of credit all over again. We also had $29,000 left over from the sale of our house that disappeared for meth within just a few months. I was completely strung out. I would get so paranoid about having everything for that lab around. I began hiding it in different places and eventually traded off different items, glassware, chemicals etc. for more dope.

My parents told us we had to move out so we rented a house. By the end of 1997 had moved again and had every charge card maxed out. I was so sick of what meth had reduced me to. I hated myself. We were completely bankrupt. We had even moved out of Joplin trying to get away from it. I was driving to Carl Junction to my welding shop, which was basically just a tweek shop. At one point I almost even called the law on myself. I had been up for several days and the only items that I had left from my lab was the bottle of anhydrous and about 150 grams of lithium wire that I had hidden in a jar of mineral oil. There were all kinds of thinners and solvents in my paint booth. So during this time I was extremely paranoid and I believed that when I would leave my shop that someone was somehow getting in. I thought that they were somehow going to set me up. So one morning I was cutting steel and the sparks were flying and they ignited the wall after I had left. At home and I got a call that my shop was on fire. I hadn't realized that it was the sparks smoldering and eventually catching fire.

Immediately I thought someone had gotten in and was cooking dope. I thought they set a fire to set me up. I was calling a lawyer and trying to explain that someone had broken into my shop was cooking dope and set it on fire. Then I almost called the police. Thank God that I didn't. But I came real close to turning myself in on accident and there was enough evidence in there to get me real good. By December of 1997 I had closed my shop. We basically had no money, nowhere to go and we were behind on the rent.

My parents owned 275 acres about 30 miles from Joplin. They had a new house in the woods. There was also a small farmhouse at the front of the property. At the end of December 1997 I had gone down to the karate studio where I took karate. The couple who taught me were also Christians. They prayed with me and helped to get some of the spirits off me long enough for me to see daylight. I also want to thank them for the years that I was a paranoid basket case. They always listened and tried to help me. In January 1998 my wife was 8 months pregnant, the rent was due and I had no job. I convinced my parents into letting us move into that small farmhouse which was perfect for us at the time. I was staying off the meth and my dad had let me start working for him again. On February 15, 1998 my wife gave birth to our second daughter Natalie. This was also the first time we attended Shoal Creek Revival Church.

During the next several months I used meth a handful of times. I never bought any but would snort a line here and there. During this time I was still smoking pot on a daily basis and drinking heavily. I kept all this hidden while we attended church. As 1999 rolled around I began using meth again whenever I could get away with it. I used on weekends or days I knew I had off work. My church attendance was dropping off. By May 1999 I was using again almost every week. Things around the house were falling apart. I was becoming paranoid again. By this time I knew that I didn't want to play the game of running around looking for dope. I also knew where I could get red phosphorous by the pound. So I ordered a pound and waited for it to arrive. I didn't know it but Daella had refused this pound of red through the mail several times. We had gone out of town and she told me this and I thought well they'll just send it back and I won't worry about it. The day we got back, Daella went to the grocery store and UPS delivered my pound of red. I signed for it. I stashed it in the woods. Now I had a bargaining chip. I headed out the next day with about a quarter pound to trade for some finished dope. The first place I went was a good friend who lived down on the river. I had been down there a couple of days before. I knew I could work out something with him. His wife answered the door and said that he couldn't come to the door. I went to another friends house. So I left the red with him and said that I'd come back tomorrow and we'd work out the exact details. This was on June 23.

On June 25, 1999 everything came to a head. I had been up on meth for about seven or eight days. I came home and was accusing my wife of all kinds of things. All five of our kids were there. They could tell I was tweaked out. By this time I had become violent and had Daella cornered in the garage. She slapped me and I grabbed her and shoved her forcibly into the car. We ended up back in the house. She had called our pastor, Charlie Brown without me knowing about it. About 15 minutes later Steve Jackson and his sister Kristi Harvill showed up in her van. Steve came to the door and told me he needed something welded. We were talking, while Daella and the kids went out the back door and left in the van.

The devil was all over me by now. My family was gone. I knew I would lose my job so I told myself I might as well go pick up more meth. I got in my pickup, went to the liquor store, got some beer and was driving back to my house. When I drove up Pastor Charlie Brown, Bill Harvill and my brother were standing outside. I honked and drove by. They Holy Spirit was telling me to go back. Thank God I listened. I had almost listened to those voices that drive every addict to a destructive end. Thank God for the Holy Spirit.

As I turned my truck around the battle inside my mind was relentless. One voice was saying, "Head back to Joplin. Everything's ruined. Your family is gone. Go get more dope. You've already made a deal for more so go pick it up." The other voice was saying "Just turn around. Everything will be okay." I pulled into the garage. Bill, Charlie and David, my brother, followed me into the house. We all sat down. I asked them sarcastically if they wanted a beer. By this time the demons inside me had taken over. I just sat and listened and gave back answers that made no sense. Everyone could see we were getting nowhere.

My wife had called my pastor who contacted Kristi Harvill. She found Bill getting ready for a little league game. Charlie told Bill that I was in trouble. He said I was on meth and getting violent. Bill thought, "Great-that's just what everyone wants to hear." So he told Charlie that he'd finish up and head right over. Bill said as he was standing there by his truck when the Holy Spirit anointed him. He spoke just a few words in tongues but it felt like someone dumped a bucket of cold ice water down his back.

We still were getting nowhere. Bill asked Charlie and my brother to go outside so he could speak to me alone. Bill said "Steve let's put Jesus back in control." I would give him some answer that was off the wall and didn't make sense. He would ask me if I knew who was in control and was controlling me. I would say "Yes, I know. The devil's in control right now and he hates you Bill." This went on for 15 or 20 minutes. Finally Bill said "Steve will you let me pray for you?" I agreed. Bill laid his hands on me and didn't say one word in English. He spoke in other tongues and the awesome power of the Holy Spirit fell and expelled the darkness in me. It was almost unbelievable. The methed-out lunatic melted into a pile of mush and the real me returned. When the Holy Ghost comes on the scene there is great power and complete authority over the demonic world. I sat there with that pile of demonic bricks off me. Bill convinced me to go to bed. He took my beer, which I gave over willingly. My family came back about 20 minutes later and I went to bed.

The next day was Saturday June 26. Bill came by to check on me. He told me he had arranged with my parents, which were also my employers, for me to be off work and go to our yearly church youth summer camp. It began on Sunday. I told Bill that I still had about 3/4 pound of red phosphorus hidden out in the woods. So we hiked out there and gave it a big toss into the wind. After Bill and I came back out of the woods, he began to tell me the only way I would make it was to give my entire life to the Lord. He said I had to become chained to the tree of Calvary. He used an example of a large oak tree in our backyard. He said my life could be changed if I would allow Christ to chain me to the tree of Calvary, instead of being chained to the world of methamphetamine. At the same time there was a voice in my head that was saying as soon as Bill leaves go get your chainsaw and cut down that tree. The devil was trying to steal the words that would set me free. Mark 4:15 says ". . .Satan cometh immediately, and taketh away the word that was sown in their hearts." John 10:10 says "The thief cometh not, but for to steal, and to kill, and to destroy: I am come that they might have life, and that they might have it more abundantly." We must understand that this is a spiritual battle I was facing. The next day we went to our morning service then left for camp that afternoon. I was still somewhat under the control of demons and unclean spirits. When we arrived at camp the sleeping arrangements were not what I had wanted and I was looking for any reason to be able to get out of there. I remember telling my wife "Let's leave. I don't want to stay

45

here." But the Holy Spirit was prompting me to stay. Thank God I did.

The Sunday night service included a ministering team from Texas. His testimony was how he had been delivered years earlier from drugs. I went down front during the altar call. Almost immediately I was slain in the Spirit. Several of the adult males members in our church were casting demons out of me in the Name of Jesus. I was spitting some unclean spirits out and breathing others out. It was getting the job done. One of the men, Jim Chapman, from the leading of the Holy Ghost said, "Let's take this show on the road." He meant let's take Steve up the hill away from everyone else and continue. Once upon the hill, they laid me back down and continued to cast demons out. I can remember growling while some came out and trying to bang my head on the ground while others came out. Eventually I said, "Let me up. I need to puke and I believe more came out as I vomited uncontrollably. I experienced a peace and release that was awesome to say the least.

The next night, was a great night of ministry also. I was receiving things from the Lord and He was laying the groundwork for my total deliverance. It was at camp that Billy Ray birthed the idea for this book. Tuesday came and the evening service was again an unbelievable night of the Holy Spirit moving and changing lives. After the evening service, around 10:00 p.m. I was down by the cabins and many of the male youth wanted to go swimming so I told them after the girls were done swimming, so I would take them. We waited until 11:00 p.m. The girls came up the hill and about a dozen young men and myself went down to the swimming pool. For some reason we just stood there and didn't get it. They said, "let's just go back to the cabins and go to bed." So we went back up the hill.

I went in my cabin and did a Bible study with the four young men in the room. Then it was lights out. During this time this voice in my head kept repeating, "Where's Phil?" Phil Jackson was the other adult counselor who was in our cabin. I hadn't seen him since the evening service. I laid down on my bunk but the Holy Spirit was relentless. "Where's Phil? Get up and go find him." So finally I got up and started looking around the camp. At first I went in the cafeteria but he wasn't there. As I walked out of cafeteria, I could see down into the open air tabernacle where the services were held. It was getting close to midnight. I could see that there were several people still down there and something very unusual was going on. I watched from up on the hill for a few minutes with another brother in Christ. Then I said "I'm going down there."

As I approached the sanctuary I could see that something awesome and almost unexplainable was happening. Just as I entered the building a sort of pleasant pressure hit me in the back of the head. The anointing was so strong it was overwhelming. People were in the Spirit in a way I, and everyone there, had never seen or experienced before. All I can say is that there was an unseen river that was flowing through that building and actually lifted some people off their seats. One young woman, Lisa Swank, was actually before the throne of God in the Spirit and was answering questions that our Pastor Charlie Brown was asking. The anointing and ministering was moving around the room to different people.

I remember being jealous of what God was doing in the other individuals. I remember being down on my knees worshipping God. The next thing I knew I was out in the Spirit, wrapped around this wooden pew on my back in a most contorted angle. But I couldn't move. No matter how I tried I couldn't move. I could still hear what was going on around me but the Spirit of God was holding me. I could sense the others there as the river of God flowed towards me. I was swept into this anointing. A chain of intercession began that later I'm told, was like nothing had never seen. Pastor wrote later that it was like a spiritual life rope to preserve and rescue me literally at times from the pit of Hell. He said there was such an intensity that they were all bewildered and prayed incessantly to beat the strong holds that were to be cleansed in the river, out for good.

I can only remember pieces of this. Pastor would write later that instructions came like a machine gun from Lisa. "Put the Word under his head and in his hand and speak to me." I remember fighting this. My hand did not want to hold the Bible. As I went deeper, peace began to manifest and my countenance showed it. They were still battling yet as the enemy pulled in the spirit realm. The life chain was too strong for that and rest came after many moments.

Joy and celebration began. I can remember finally lying there with a Bible under my head and one in my hand. I could open my eyes but was unable to move. When I finally could move, my spirit was dying and thirsting to be fed with the Word of God. I opened the Bible in my hand as I lay there and it was like my mind could read at an unbelievable rate. It was the most peaceful and serene feeling I have ever experienced. For a long time I couldn't move. Then the spirit released me to sit up. I was told later that this life chain to me had gone on approximately 45 minutes. Many doubt that there is a God or that He cares for each one of us. I can guarantee you there is a Creator and Almighty God who loves you and wants you to spend eternity with Him.

The days following camp were some of the toughest days I have ever faced. I immediately went back to work. I found myself going by Bill's house almost daily to share with him the battle that was going on in my mind. For example one day I had been working construction. I was being tormented all day about going and picking up the dope or money from the last trade. I had made with the red phosphorous. I told Bill I wanted to get the money that was owed to me. At that time I probably would have gotten more dope instead of the money and I knew it. I was finding out that I needed someone who I could just be honest with about my feelings. The day I told him about the money that was owed, this is what he said to me. "Steve, you've been saved. You've been washed in the blood of the Lamb. You've been saved and set free." Psalms 103:12 says "As far as the east is from the west, so far hath he removed our transgressions [sins] from us. Bill began to tell me I was no longer a player in the old world and give up my position in the drug world. I had to give up the money and the dope and let it go. Because God had let it go, I had to let it go. This was very hard for me because the old me didn't want to let anyone get anything over on me. Second Corinthians 5:17 says "Therefore if any man be in Christ, he is a new creature: old things are passed away; behold, all things are become new." When I visited Bill we would end in prayer and he would rebuke the devil off of me. I soon found out this was what helped. It was the prayer and taking authority over the demons that had been driving me for so long. The Word of God was setting me free. Matthew 4:4 says "... It is written, Man shall not live by bread alone, but by every word that proceedeth out of the mouth of God." When I was being attacked I could use scripture to fight the battle. I memorized scripture and taped different ones up in my car and house. The very first one I memorized was Psalm 32:7: "Thou art my hiding place; thou shalt preserve me from trouble; thou shalt compass me about with songs of deliverance. Selah." You have to find someone that will care about your life and take the time to listen and council you, the way that Bill did for me— someone that you can be truthful with about anything. Bill said the reason I was staying set free was that I was truthful and not ashamed of my thoughts. So I would share all the wacked out things that were going through my mind. "Confess your faults one to another, and pray one for another, that ye may be healed. The effectual fervent prayer of a righteous man availeth much" (James 5:16).

Some of these things have worked and will work in yours or your loved ones life. You can't find something unless your looking for it. I pray that you will begin to look, God will bring someone across your path. They will be a person that you can trust and confide in, who won't condemn you. They will pray and tell you about the things of God in a language that you can understand. Someone that is born again and serving God.

One thing that helped me was when I got involved at Shoal Creek Revival Church. I became a servant to the needs of the church and others. I always tried to be at any work days even just to sweep the floor. You must become involved with working for the Kingdom of God. If you're in prison, you can get involved by helping your chaplain and be involved in every Christian activity. Get involved in prayer groups, church services or just reach out in love to your fellow man. Since the Lord has set me free, I'd like to say everything has been perfect, but that would be a lie. I've made many mistakes, but I'm not going to quit. There is no price that can be put on having a life again. I want to encourage you to never give in, never believe the devils lies and to stand strong until the Lord's return!

The Eyewitness

Second Peter chapter 1 and verse 16 says "for we have not followed cunningly devised fables, when we made known unto you the power and coming of our Lord Jesus Christ, but were eyewitnesses of his majesty."

Before I continue on with this book, I have to tell you of what I have been an eye witness to. The definition of an eyewitness is, one who has himself seen a specific thing happen. I've been an eyewitness of God beginning to work in my life, to shape me in to someone that can be of service to him. I have been an eyewitness to his power and presence at the youth camp where the chains were broken off of me. I have been in a lot of different situations in my life, but that one takes the cake is knowing that there is a true living God, the one of the Bible.

After the experience at camp, I slowly began to walk out of the person that I was. During this time Bill Harvill had begun to tell me that I should write a book about the sorcery of methamphetamine. At first, I just kind of laughed and said Bill if I ever write a book I'll put our picture on the back cover. So the weeks were passing by, and Bill would continue to encourage me about writing the book that is now called *Meth = Sorcery Know the Truth*, he would say that the Holy Spirit was telling him to tell me this.

So a few more weeks went by and one Sunday night I was going to give my testimony at our church. Praise and worship was going on, and I was getting in to praising the Lord, I had my eyes shut and all of a sudden I could see myself in a boxing ring and I was fighting this guy and the bell rang, I ran back to my corner and there was Bill yelling at me what to do. Then bam it was gone, I thought man that was wild. Later that night I told Daella about it and I began to seek the Lord on what it meant. I had never had a vision before and was quite intrigued by it. The Holy Spirit revealed to me that the vision was meant for me to listen to Bill about the writing of the book. So I was an eyewitness to this happening.

During the days following Bill and I would make an outline and I would go home. Many nights the Holy Spirit would prompt me to get up and start writing in a notebook. Some nights He would get me up around midnight and I would write to the wee hours of the morning. It was kind of ironic because this is when before I would be up freaking out on meth. As the period of time went on in which that book was wrote, I was an eye-witness to several things.

First on several occasions there was an evil presence that would come into my house and try to scare me with voices in my head about not writing the book and that they were going to kill me. I found that I had to stand up and combat these with the Word of God and then one time the Holy Spirit told me to tell them that if they were going to kill me to do it now. Guess what they haven't got the job done yet.

The second thing that I was witness to was on two occasions while writing in my notebook when I would finish a page, it would roll up by itself, like a scroll. At first this kind of freaked me out and I would holler at Daella and say watch this, I would continue to write, finish a page and it would roll up by itself. To me that was quite a supernatural event from God.

More time went on and I was nearing the completion of the book and I had no cover for it. Another Sunday night in prayer, a certain woman in our congregation was in the spirit on the floor and several people were down praying with her. I went over and began to pray and bam in my head I saw a big dark demonic figure in a black shroud standing in front of a witch's kettle, he had a big stick that he was stirring it with. In the kettle or pot there was dozens of hands sticking out of the brew. I was looking at this like I was standing to the front of this thing. Down below the pot there were thousands of people stacked on top of each other with their hands in the air, worshipping this thing. All I could see was the backs of the people and that they were shredded and in anguish. After that night I knew I had the cover for *Meth = Sorcery Know the Truth.*

I have been an eyewitness to these things and then them coming to pass. I have found out that God had a purpose for these things happening, and I found out it wasn't about me but it was about Him and How He wants His people set free from this bondage. Before I close this chapter, I want to tell you one more thing that I have been an eyewitness to. I have witnessed the Lord continuing to forgive me and to encourage me to go on. Of Him wanting a relationship with me and I have seen the Power of His Word, that His Word is alive.

Prophecy of Sorcery

What I want to do in this chapter is lay out what the Bible has to say about sorcery in the end times. First let's look at several definitions of sorcery, now while I don't want to repeat much of my first book *Meth = Sorcery Know The Truth*, I feel it is imperative that we continue to discuss this now. The Greek biblical definition of sorcery is *pharmakoi* or *pharmakon*, which translates in English as pharmacy or drugs. In the Greek it means the cutting of herbs and mixing of ingredients, which are potions. it also means poisoner. Now in the Hebrew the word sorcery translates as *Kesheph*, meaning witchcrafts, to whisper a magical spell, to mutter magical words or incantations. it also means to enchant to be a sorcerer. So basically sorcery is the mixing of a potion and whispering of spells. The mixing of a potion is exactly what is going on inside meth labs. How about poisoner, most of the ingredients used to cook meth are poisons and acids and flammable substances. Let's look now at what the encyclopedia definition says about sorcery and sorcerers. First it says that sorcerers are regarded as ordinary people driven by deplorable urges such as malice, envy, or revenge. It also says that to perform sorcery, it demands no special personal attributes and is practiced by anyone who can acquire the necesasry ingredients. Finally that sorcery is the work of ordinary persons using deliberate techniques and means familiar to other adult members of the community. Make a comparison with meth production in your community with these facts. The encyclopedia also says that all sorcery and witchcrafts have four or five recurring elements and they are as follows.

Five Recurring Elements of Sorcery

1. Performance of ritual = This encompasses the entire meth production process.

2. Use of material substances = These are the chemicals and ingredients used in meth production.

3. Objects that symbolic significance = These are the beakers or mason jars, it can even be a five gallon plastic bucket, thermometers, tubing, magnetic stirrers. These objects are symbolic to the person performing the cook.

4. Utterance of a closely prescribed spell = These are the different recipes, that are closely followed each time.

5. A prescribed condition of the performer or cook = This condition includes the false sense of worth, thoughts of power and control over people, thoughts of never having to work again. Total obedience to meth.

Now let's look at the dictionary definition of sorcery, it says, The use of supernatural power over others through the assistance of spirits, witchcraft. You could also say tampering with the powers of darkness. This is where the whispering comes into play. First Samuel 15:23 says, "For rebellion is as the sin of witchcraft . . ." Methamphetamine has been designed for a certain purpose. This design is for a person to mimic Satan, in all out rebellion against everything that is good for our lives. Genesis 3:1 says that the serpent was more subtle than any beast of the field. What is more subtle than having millions of people performing sorcery and witchcraft and not even knowing it.

Ephesians 5:11, "And have no fellowship with the unfruitful works of darkness, but rather expose them." You see it is our job to bring to light the things of darkness. Exposing Methamphetamine for what it really is, that's what this book is all about.

The following scriptures are from the book of Revelation. Revelation deals with the events that will take place before the return of Jesus Christ. Revelation is talking about the end times as we know it. Revelation 9:21 says, "Nether repented they of their murders, nor of their sorceries."

Revelation 18:23 says, "And the light of a candle shall shine no more at all in the; and the voice of the bridegroom and of the bride shall be heard no more at all in thee; for thy merchants were the great men of the earth; for by thy sorceries were all nations deceived."

Revelation 21:8 says, "But the fearful and the unbelieving, and the abominable, and murderers, and whoremongers, and sorcerers, and idolaters, and all liars, shall have their part int he lake which burneth with fire and brimstone; which is the second death."

Revelation 22:15 says, "For without are dogs and sorcerers, whoremongers, murderers, idolaters, and whosoever loveth and maketh a lie."

Revelation lists sorcerers and sorceries four times, more than any other book of the Bible. So what is God saying to you and I? In the end times there is going to be wide spread sorcery, unlike ever before on planet earth. Up until now, there was not a fulfillment of sorcery. The sorcery that the Bible is talking about is methamphetamine production in our society, and the pharmaceutical industry. Let us look at this a little further in the book of Isaiah chapter 47. This deals with the judgement on Babylon, which is a picture of the world. Isaiah 47 now portrays Babylon as a deposed queen who can do no more than sit in the dust. In this passage Babylon is portrayed as a naked slave girl reduced to sitting in the dust. She is no longer the lady (mistress) of kingdoms. This same imagery is found in Revelation, where Babylon is called "The Great Whore." Revelation 17:1, 19:2, and 18:3.

Isaiah 47 is an imagery of the book of Revelations. So let us look at what Isaiah 47 says about sorcery. Isaiah 47:9 says, "But these two things shall come to thee, in a moment in one day, the loss of children and widowhood; they shall come upon thee in their perfection for the multitude of thy sorceries and for the great abundance of thine enchantments." The next chapter will break down this scriptures in Hebrew.

Now let us look at Isaiah 47:12, "Stand now with thine enchantments, and with the multitudes of thy sorceries, wherein thou hast labored from thy youth; if so be thou shalt be able to profit, if so be thou mayest prevail." Again I encourage you to read all of Isaiah 47, it mirrors Revelation and the sorcery that will be taking place in these end times.

Malachi is the last book of the Old Testament, it was written approximately 2,400 years ago. Chapter 3 is talking about the approaching day of judgment or the end times. Malachi 3:5 says, "And I will come near to you to judgment, and I will be a swift witness agaisnt the sorcerers, and against the adulterers, and against the false swearers, and against those that appress the hireling in his wages, the widow, and the fatherless, and that turn aside the stranger from his right, and fear not Me, saith the Lord of Hosts." So God is listing out things that will be swiftly judged. At one time I was praying and asking God why He listed sorcerers first. The answer I got was, that in the world of sorcery asnd methamphetamine, there is every abomination that God hates. So all of the sins that separate man from God are entwined together in witchcraft and sorcery. First Samuel 15:23 says, "For rebellion is as the sin of witchcraft." So what a person needs to understand is that rebellion is basically what Lucifer or Satan did when he wanted to be like God. Methamphetamine has been demonically developed for these end times to make a person act like and do the will of satan. Everyone who is involved with meth at one time or another becomes a dealer to support their habit. Some are dealing huge quantities and are involved in multi-million dollar meth operations, while others are selling 1/4 grams ($25) to support their own daily habit. Regardless where a person fits into this broad spectrum of dealers, a treacherous blow is being dealt to our society. In the book of Isaiah chapter 24, often called the Little Apocolypse because it looks beyond the immediate judgments of the tribulation period. Isaiah is also a book that deals with the end times and in 24:16-19 it says, "From the uttermost parts of the earth have we heard songs even glory to the righteous. But I said, My leaness, my leaness woe unto me! the treacherous dealers have dealt treacherously; yea, the treacherous dealers have dealt very treacherously. Fear and the pit, and the snare, are upon thee, O inhabitant of the earth. And it shall come to pass, that he who fleeth from the noise of the fear shall fall into the pit; and he that cometh up out of the midst of the pit shall be taken in the snare: for the windows from on high are open, and the foundations of the earth do shake."

Methamphetamine is being used in these end times to bewitch it's users, to use them, to destroy lives, families, to blunt a persons emotions to a point where doing all of this destruction has no effect on them. To make an army of meth zombies that are willing to do anything for more meth. Methamphetamine is breeding sorcerers. In the book of Acts chapter 13:10, talks about what a sorcerer is and says, "O full of all sbutility and all mischief, thou child of the devil, thou enemy of all righteousness, wilt thou not cease to pervert the right ways of the Lord?"

So how will methamphetmine be used in these end times? First let's look at a predecessor to the antichrist, his name was Adolph Hitler. One of the predominate recipes used in meth production today is called the Nazi-method, which uses anhydrous ammonia. Is is said that Hitler used this method to produce methamphetmine to feed to his soldiers so they could kill day and night. To make a fighting machine that was ruthless, a soldier whose conscience was seared and one who would kill with no emotion. In the book of Revelation chapter 13 verse 15-17 says that "And he had power to give life unto the image of the beast, that the image of the beast should both speak, and cause that as many as would not worship the image of the beast should be killed. And he causeth all, both small and great, rich and poor, free and bond, to receive a mark in their right hand, or in their foreheads. And that no man might buy or sell, save he that had the mark, or the name of the beast, or the number of his name."

There is a day coming when anyone left on planet Earth will be required to worship the image of the beast or be killed. They will also be required to take a mark, or basically a small microscopic computer chip in the hand or their forehead, or be killed. This mark or chip will enable satan to be able to monitor a person's every move, both personal, financial, as well as physical location. But a person shouldn't worry about his own physical death, especially if you have accepted the Lord as your Savior. Whatever you do never, let me say again never ever take this mark from the beast. Revelation 14:9-11 says "And the third angel followed them saying with a loud voice, if any man worship the beast and his image, and receive his mark, in his forehead, or in his hand. The same shall drink of the wine of the wrath of God, which is poured out without mixture into the cup of indignation, and he shall be tormented with fire and brimstone in the presence of the holy angels, and in the presence of the Lamb. And the smoke of their torment ascendeth up forever and ever: and they have no rest day nor night, who worship the beast and his image, and whosoever receiveth the mark of his name."

There will be millions who will not worship the beast, nor take his mark. These people will most likely be hunted day and night, by an army or militia that is on methamphetamine. There will possibly be bands of men and woman, meth-addicts, who will also participate in the capture and execution of the people who will not receive the mark. I'm sure they will be rewarded with more methamphetamine. The only objection, to hunt and kill Christians. Understand even though these may be killed and hunted, they have the victory, not the devil. Revelation 15:2 says, "And I saw as it were a sea of glass mingled with fire; and them that had gotten the victory over the beast, and over his image, and over his mark, and over the number of his name, stand on the sea of glass, having the harps of God." People everywhere need to stand up for the things of God and do everything they can to reach the lost, while there is still time. To do everything in our abilities to tell the truth about methamphetamine and the sorcery that underlies it. Methamphetamine could be the greatest tool of Satan in these end times. But thank God if you are reading this book and are trapped, you can be set free. Colossians 1:12-14, 16-18, 21, 22 says, "Giving thanks unto the Father, which hath made us meet to be partakers of the inheritance of the saints in light. Who hath delivered us from the power of darkness, and hath translated us into the kingdom of his dear Son. In whom we have redemption through the blood, even the forgiveness of sins. For by him were all things created, that are in heaven, and that are in earth, visible and invisible, whether they be thrones, or dominions, or principalities, or powers: all things were created by him and for him: And he is before all things and by him all things consist. And he is the head of the body, the church: who is the beginning, the first born from the dead; that in all things he might have the pre-eminence. And you, that were sometime alienated and enemies in your mind by wicked works, yet now hath he reconciled. In the body of his flesh through death, to present you holy and unblameable and unreproveable in his sight:" He did it for us! Jesus did it for you and me.

Batsa
The Perfection of Methamphetamine

What is the perfection of methamphetamine? What does meth do that no other drug before it was able to do? It fulfills the Word of God! Let me explain, No other drug in history can compare with the destruction that meth holds, not only for the user, but also for the basic family unit, anyone who is around will be affected and also society as a whole. The perfection as used in Isaiah 47:9 in the Hebrew translates as *batsa*, the main thrust of this word is tearing something to pieces, ripping, breaking, unrighteous gain, to rob, to plunder, greedy, given over to covetous. Remember now that the entire chapter 47 of Isaiah deals with the end times and the sorcery that will be taking place. What I'd like to do is take a look at the true picture of meth, described out Isaiah 47:9 Broken down into the Hebrew.

Isaiah 47:9 says, "But these two things shall come to thee in a moment in one DAY, the LOSS OF CHILDREN, and widowhood: they shall come upon thee in their PERFECTION for the multitude of thy SORCERIES, and for the great abundance of thine ENCHANTMENTS."

1. DAY = *Yowm* - A point in time, when or on some particular day, could be 24 hours, or a specific point in time, or a year. In the Aramaic it means in the latter days.
2. LOSS OF CHILDREN = *Sh>Kowl* - Bereavement, childlessness, loss of children, ABANDONMENT, the condition of one who has been left by everyone.
3. PERFECTION = *Batsa* - The main thrust of this word is tearing something to complete pieces, ripping, breaking, unrighteous gain, to rob, to plunder, greedy, given over to complete covetous and idolatry.

4. SORCERIES = *Kesheph* in Hebrew *Kesheph* = witchcrafts, to whisper a magical spell, TO WHISPER, to mutter magical words or incantations, to enchant, to be a sorcerer Kesheph is very similar to Nachash out of Genesis 3:1 for serpent to hiss an incantation, to whisper, a magic spell. *Pharmakon* or *Phamakoi* in the Greek The cutting of herbs and the MIXING OF A POTION, POISONER.

5. ENCHANTMENTS = *Cheber* - to tie a magic knot. It means a COMMUNITY, a SOCIETY, a company, a spell, a charm.

So basically Isaiah 47:9 is saying those involved in sorcery or methamphetamine, whichever you want to call it, where each person will reach a point in time, this time will be different in each person's life. It might take 15 years or it could be the first time you stick a needle in your arm. Each individual's life will be a different point in time. Where you will lose your children and you yourself will be left in the position of total abandonment, the condition of one who has been left by everyone. The perfection of this world of meth or sorcery, will be to literally tear your life to pieces, to destroy your family, your parents and everyone around you. It's also to tear your mind to pieces, your body, and make you a carbon copy of the devil himself. This sorcery will be performed by the mixing of a potion, a poisoner. (METH LABS) This potion or meth, will break down a spiritual gate in your being, so that a demonic whispering can take place, to drive you insane. You will speak into existence your own doom. These demonic incantations whispered to you by demons, these lies straight from the pit of hell, will become your truth. You will rape, rob, and pillage your surroundings all because some demon told you to. All of this will take place in order to tie your life into a magic knot, and make you part of a society or a community known as the world of meth. So I'll ask the question, Why is methamphetamine the way it is in our society? The answer is because the Word of God says so! Methamphetamine is not going away, in fact it is spreading out of control.

Second Timothy 3:13 talking about the end times says "But evil men and seducers shall wax worse and worse, deceiving and being deceived." Let's look further at 2 Timothy 3:1-5 says "This know also that in the last days perilous times shall come. For men shall be lovers of their own selves covetous, boasters, proud, blasphemers, disobedient to parents, unthankful, unholy, without natural affection, truce breakers, false accusers, incontinent, fierce, despisers of those that are good. Traitors, heady highminded, lovers of pleasures more than lovers of God; Having a form of godliness, but denying the power thereof: from such turn away.

Let's skip down a couple of verses to 2 Timothy 3:8 says, "Now as Jannes and Jambres withstood Moses, so do these also resist the truth: men of corrupt minds, reprobate concerning the faith." Remember this is talking about the end times. Jannes and Jambres were sorcerers in Pharoah's court. More sorcery in end time scripture, God is very clear about sorcery. Verse 9 says, "But they shall proceed no further: for their folly shall be manifest unto all men, as theirs also was. If you or someone you love is trapped in meth, or maybe your reading this in jail and you want to be set free or see them set free, the first step in all of this is surrendering your life to the Lord." Romans 10:9 says, "That if thou shalt confess with thy mouth the Lord Jesus, and shalt believe in thine heart that God hath raised him from the dead, thou shalt be saved. For with the heart man believeth unto righteousness; and with the mouth confession is made unto salvation."

The Branches of Sorcery

What are the branches of sorcery? There are many, now while we've been looking at only methamphetamine there are many others in our society today. Let's take a look at a popular drug on the scene today called ecstasy or mdma. On the street it goes by Adam, Bean, E, Ecstasy, M, Roll, X, or XTC. So what is this drug? It's chemical name is (3-4-methylenedioxymethamphetamine). It is synthetic amphetamine, with hallucinogenic properties. It is a branch of meth, plain and simple. This drug is being used to attack mainly our youth at party called raves. Now let me tell you what I know about ecstasy, over the years I probably used X 50 to 100 times. This drug after taken produces an effect of total well being, it gives the user the mind set of being able to deal with any situation in a controlled and loving manner. It also breaks down all inhibitions in the realm of sexuality. This is probably its greatest use. Let me tell you a story of one particular incident when I was under the influence of Ecstasy. I had taken a hit a few hours earlier and was on my way out to a friends house, who owned two pit bulls. Now usually these dogs would act ferocious with me and could smell that I was afraid of them. It was well known that these dogs were mean and would bite. Under the influence of ecstasy I jumped into there pen and proceeded to wrestle them. Thank God, they just played with me. So what I'm saying is this drug is very deceptive, it will convince your thinking into where you think you are in complete control of every situation. This is just a short example of its dangers.

I believe that most all of the street drugs that are out there are a form of sorcery including heroin, cocaine, especially crack cocaine, LSD, PCP, and all the new designer drugs that are coming onto the drug scene. The difference with these and meth is that, meth takes the performance of the actual act of sorcery into our society at a unprecedented level, unlike any other drug before. This drug is a form of idolatry that is taken to a whole other level of idol worship. Before we discuss some of the other forms of sorcery in our society, let's look closer at this idolatry of meth and its stronghold over the user.

The Stronghold

Why does meth have such a stronghold over people lives? What is it that makes this drug so different from all the previous drugs addicting our society? Why is it spreading so fast across America and the world? Why is there such supernatural evidence and occurrences in the world of meth that are clearly demonic? For a minute, I want you to imagine that you're a meth addict, and that you and I have been awake for a couple of weeks with absolutely no sleep. Let's say we're at your house and I'm getting ready to leave. So I'm walking out the door and I turn to you and said I'm leaving now, but I'll be back later to visit or get you. So now I'm gone, the next day I call or come by and you are freaking out. You tell me that I came back to your house a few hours after I'd left. I knocked at the door and you let me in, and we were doing more dope and drinking for a couple of hours. Then you turned around to make us another drink, now turning back to hand me my drink, I vanish, dissipate into thin right before your eyes. Now back in the other end of the telephone, I laugh and tell you I was never there. That same night I had sent out an image of myself to several locations. While I know this sounds impossible, this is just one every day occurrence in the world of meth.

Quickly I'll give another. Recently I was talking with a woman who was designing a web page about the dangers of meth. She had recently been interviewing a group of people who are heavily involved in meth. These people told her both individually, as well as when the group was together that these small men were appearing to them, out of thin air. They were beginning to communicate with them and had even named them calling them the artesians. So what is it that people who are on meth really seeing? What is it that makes lies become truth? A place where your behavior mimics schizophrenia. A place of unbelievable sexual perversion. A place where innocent blood is shed. A place of torment and self-mutilation. A place where audio and visual hallucinations are as real as you and I. I'm talking about a direct hook up with the demonic spiritual realm. To a meth addict there life becomes a complete sell out and worship unlike anything there has ever been. It consumes every waking minute which is continuous for weeks on end. Everyday people have to deal with life's situations, even someone living for God, has to take care of their daily business. Then we find time to worship God and study His Word, and to seek His perfect will for our lives. Not so with meth addiction, everything revolves around more meth day and night! This is why God hates meth or sorcery, whichever you want to call it. An addicts entire being is turned over to this witchcraft and rebellion. This continuous seeking for meth and the things of meth is what opens up the entire spectrum of the evil supernatural realm, where satan and his army can lead and guide an addict and their family to a place to kill, steal, and destroy them. Just like everything that belongs to the devil, is a counterfeit meth is a counterfeit of what it feels like to walk in the spirit with Almighty God. The stronghold against the user can be overcome.

Second Corinthians 10:3-5 says, "For though we walk in the flesh, we do not war after the flesh (For weapons of our warfare are not carnal, but mighty through God to the pulling down of strongholds;) Casting down imaginations and every high thing that exalteth itself against the knowledge of God, and bringing into captivity every thought to the obedience of Christ." Before I continue, I want to say to the person sitting in jail that you can be completely set free, from the strangle hold of meth. The first step is to get things right between you and Almighty God. This reconciliation comes through his Son, the Lord Jesus Christ! Realizing that this is not a game, that where you will spend eternity depends on your decision. John 14:6, "Jesus said unto them, I am the way, the truth, and life: no man cometh unto the Father, but by me." Right now you can be certain of your eternal home! John 14:2, 3 says, "In my Father's house are many mansions: if it were not so, I would have told you. I go to prepare a place for you. And if I go and prepare a place for you, I will come again, and receive you unto myself; that where I am, there you may be also." All you have to do is from your heart ask the Lord to forgive you for your sins believe that he died on the cross for you, and that He is the Son of God Tell Him you accept Him as your personal saviour and to come into your heart. Praise God! If you prayed this prayer your slate has been completely wiped clean! Get this your name is now written in the Lambs Book of Life in Heaven! This is just the first step of a new life, from this day forward let the peace of God rule your life.

Crack Cocaine

In the previous paragraph I listed many of the other drugs that are on the scene today and I said that crack-cocaine was high up on the list of sorcery, let me explain why. Now, while crack was never my thing, let me tell you what I've found to be true. The drugs that are being produced by everyday people from all walk of life, are the most demonic. Understand that in order to make crack, a person first must have cocaine, now the next step to make it into crack is where you stack sorcery upon sorcery! It's when the cocaine is added with baking soda and rocked up into crack-cocaine that you take the act of performing the actual art of sorcery and put it into the person's hands who is rocking it up. I have dealt with several friends who were crack addicts and what I see from this drug is a period of total control and destruction, sometimes in only a matter of days!

The Giant

What I'd like to do now is look at the largest and possibly the most controlling branch of sorcery on planet earth today, the pharmaceutical industry! In these end times of planet earth as we know it there is a push from the pharmaceutical companies to get everybody on something and to control them! Now don't get me wrong I believe that there are many good medicines also, but there is a new approach being taken towards the general public and especially our children, and a very defined program that is used in most all rehabs, a regiment of bi-polar, anti-depressants and schizophrenic drugs. They are prescribing and addicting our children to Ritalin, Adderall, Desoxyn, and many other mind altering drugs, without looking at the long term consequences! What I want to know is how many doctors, nurses, teachers, principles, and so on have ever taken doses of these medications themselves to understand what actually goes on! When you are dealing with drugs in the amphetamine class for children, all they are looking for is a quick fix for a behavioral problem. When in actuality they are labeled by everyone as addicts already!

These kids are singled out in class to take medications and are labeled by everyone as addicts already! What these people who prescribe these drugs don't understand about meth and other amphetamines is at first they say low doses are safe and controllable, but what they need to know is that for someone who is taking these drugs that low doses only work for a while and the first time these kids get their hands on some crystal meth in junior high or high school they are hooked instantly, from being set up by our society their entire childhood. I myself have taken ritalin many times, and what people need to know is that the emotional blunting that takes place is very similar to methamphetamine! There is no quick fix in raising a child in today's world, if we would give these kids a dose of attention and love every time we gave them a pill, many would not need to be on these medications! There are many studies on ritalin, and good articles on alternatives to using these drugs on children, I encourage you to look for other ways to help your children, than simply medicating them. Let me tell you a story about ritalin that I heard on a major Christian talk show about a man who told of his five year old who was a hyper, happy, active little boy. Someone convinced him to put his son on ritalin for the hyperactivity, within a few months this happy, outgoing little fellows entire disposition changed, he became withdrawn and inverted. The story goes on to tell how eventually everything about this child changed so drastically that they found him in his room with a butchers knife cutting all of his stuffed animals heads off! This is only one example of the mind altering changes that go on with any type of amphetamines. What I want everyone to know is that meth, ritalin or any others in this grouping of drugs has this kind of effect on everyone who takes them mentally, they breed violence.

Matthew 19:6, 7 says, "Woe unto the world because of offenses! for it must needs that offenses come; but woe to that man by whom the offenses cometh!" The truth is the truth! There is a major push from these pharmaceutical companies to addict you and your loved ones. In 1999 IMS, a company that provides information to the pharmaceutical and health care industries, reported that the pharmaceutical industry spend $1.53 billion on direct-to-consumer advertising—up from even $1 billion just two years earlier. And that's just a fraction of their total advertising expenditure—an estimated $6.4 billion last year. You cannot turn on the television, open a magazine, or go anywhere, where you're not bombarded with some kind of ad trying to get you on some drug or that gives you a toll free number, which will hook you up with a doctor who will prescribe you that particular drug! From everything to getting an erection to social anxiety, and everything in between. The world of meth and drugs is an indicator of the season that we are living in, a time in eternal history that is being fulfilled.

The Diagnosis Is?

What is the diagnosis, how are you and your loved ones being diagnosed? The number one way that our rehabs and physicians are dealing with illegal drug users, is with legal ones? Hello? Is there anyone out there? Does anyone care?

I myself have taken quite a few of many types of pharmaceuticals and have been addicted to several before. One time I had a knee surgery and was given a certain pain killer, over the next several weeks I became more and more drawn into that little world that revolved around more and more. I even would fake falls in order to get my prescription refilled. I've also took my share of desoxyn, which is methamphetamine hydrochloride and I promise you it does the same thing as crystal meth off the streets.

Many doctors are diagnosing addicts with narcolepsy, how is this accomplished? There is a way to make the sleep tests diagnose you with these symptoms and addicts know it, and are sharing this information with each other.

What makes anyone think that exchanging one drug for another to treat the symptoms that an illegal drug has caused is the answer? From what I have gathered it is like this. Most anyone who is trying to come off alcohol or meth or any of the other man made drugs are being diagnosed bi-polar, manic depression, anti-social personality disorder, then they are put on a regiment of these legal drugs that are very addictive. People wouldn't be showing these symptoms if it wasn't for the meth and or the drugs that are being prescribed to them. Many doctors are hooked on drugs themselves. What is the one standard that medical doctors use to treat illegal drug addicts? There is no one standard. What is the number of graduating doctors each year? I'm sure that it is a large number. How many of these doctors are actually controlled by the pharmaceutical companies? How many legal drug dealers are getting their certification each day all across this world.

In Mark Jesus is dealing with a woman that had an issue of blood for 12 years. Mark 5:26-28, 34 says, "And she had suffered many things of many physicians, and had spent all that she had, and was nothing bettered, but rather grew worse. When she had heard of Jesus, came in the press behind and touched his garment. For she said, If I may touch but his clothes, I shall be whole. . . And he [Jesus] said unto her, Daughter thy faith hath made thee whole; go in peace, and be whole of this plague." There is still a great physician, who is still in the healing business! Doctors and everyone else on this planet, only know in part, including myself.

First Corinthians 13:8-10 says, "Charity (pursuit of love) never faileth: but whether there be prophecies, they shall fail; whether there be tongues, they shall cease; whether there be knowledge, it shall vanish away. For we know in part and we prophesy in part. But when that which is perfect (Jesus) is come, then that which is in part shall be done away with." Everything that you can read, study, or be diagnosed is an incomplete procedure. There is only one tangible thing on this planet that you can put your complete trust, faith and dependence on and that is the Word of God.

Let me close this chapter by saying this, I believe that there are many prescription drugs that are gifts from God and are extending peoples lives. But there are many that are destroying lives and you should seek the Lord for yourself, to find out what he would have you to do. One thing that I do know is that God deals with everyone differently and as an individual and will love you through everything that you must face.

The Root

The pharmaceutical companies are the most profitable companies on the face of the earth!

All of these branches of sorcery are run by the love of money, the bottom line with no understanding of the consequences. First Timothy 6:10 says that "For the love of money is the root of all evil: which while some coveted after, they have erred from the faith, and pierced themselves through with many sorrows." Money is not the root of all evil, but the love of it is. I want to encourage whoever is reading this to take a look at yourself, your children, your family and your surroundings. Are we setting the best example we can? Are we waging an effective war against the enemy? Are you reading this and caught in the web of addiction?

Psalm 144:1 says, "Blessed be the Lord my strength, which teacheth my hands to war and my fingers to fight!" So how can we wage a good and godly warfare? To make war against the enemy, we need to first understand that you do have a real enemy and his name is satan and his entire hoard would like to destroy you and your family. Second, realize there is a purpose for your life, and for you to prosper while you are here. We have a Savior that died for us, forget any perceived idea you have of God and the church world. Pick up the Bible and read the New Testament for yourself, don't let someone else mold your opinion for you. I'll write on this subject in a later chapter. Let's get back to waging war.

Get saved first, then you'll begin to wage war by becoming a better father or mother, a better husband or wife. Work on becoming a better worker and servant to others. Colossians 3:22, 23 says, "Servants, obey in all things your masters according to the flesh; not with eyeservice, as menpleasers; but in singleness of heart, fearing God: And whatsoever ye do, do it heartily, as to the Lord, and not unto men." Work always as if you're working for the Lord, in everything you do. Let me tell you how you can tell if you're a good servant. It's when somebody treats you like one, and how you react to that treatment. Do you get an attitude when told what to do?

To really see change in your life start seeking and meditating on the things of God. God's word if applied correctly will make the difference. It will change your life, when you begin to put the things of God before the things of you.

The Design of Sorcery

What is the purpose of sorcery, the design of its purpose? It revolves around driving a person insane. Methamphetamine in our society is driving our society and its participants to this end. I want to tell you in this chapter about the end results of meth use in a person's mental capacity. Psychiatrists make a distinction between the milder paranoid personality disorders and the more debilitating kind called delusional paranoia. The landmark of this disorder is the presence of a persistent, bizarre delusion without symptoms of any other mental disorder. These delusions are firmly held beliefs that are not true. These beliefs most of the time continue even after meth use stops, they isolate a person into a false perception of themselves and others around them. I want to tell you about five different themes that are present in the world of drugs and meth.

The most common delusion is that of persecution. They are suspicious about everything, they believe everyone is joking about them. They will try to confirm their suspicions by latching on to any speck of evidence that supports their own agenda and ignore anything to the contrary. They will usually believe that there is an elaborate plot to destroy them. They'll believe that they are being poisoned, drugged, spied upon or bugged, or the target of someone or an organization to kill them. They believe that their closest friends and family members are in on this. I used to fall into this category.

Let give you an example. This took place after I hadn't had any meth for a few months. My friend Bill Harvill had taken me on an all night fishing trip. It was about 2:00 a.m. in the morning and we were fishing. Bill decided to take us to another part of the lake to fish. It was a moonlit night as the boat sped across the water, he drove for about 20 minutes. As we drove the voices in my head began to tell me that Bill was in on, the plot to take my life, that all the other previous times I believed someone was out to get me were somehow connected to tonight's trip and that when we got to where we were going that there would appear the others who would help him accomplish my death. That he had actually brought me out here to drown me! It didn't matter that he was my friend and pastor, he was in on it too. These thoughts and feelings became so overwhelming that I couldn't distinguish reality and I began to look for a weapon or a way to crash the boat. Finally I just told Bill what I was thinking, he set my mind at ease and said if anyone was out to get me tonight that they'd have to drown him first. We ended up talking about this paranoia in detail as I began to tell him about the real world of meth.

The second theme seen frequently in the meth world is delusional jealousy. It could be a meaningless spot on clothing or a short delay in arriving home or possibly a phone call. These things are summoned up as evidence that a spouse or girlfriend is being unfaithful. You add in the perverted things and prostitution that go on in the drug world and you have a very volatile situation on your hands.

The third theme is one of fantasy, erotic delusion where this individual that they are romantically loved by another, usually someone of a high status, or well known public figure. Individuals with this type will usually write numerous letters, telephone calls, visits, and surveillance.

The fourth theme is called grandiose, these folks believe that they know something that no one else knows, or that few others know. Or that they have been endowed with special powers to perform extraordinary feats. Let me give you a few examples in this area, first many people in the meth world will go out looking for arrowheads and other artifacts. They'll have this elaborate collection that they believe are the real thing, when in actuality it's just a pile of rocks. I know people who believe that they have made great discoveries of entire mountains that they believe are giant dinosaur finds. Another lie in the world of meth is that there is a meth czar over each state who is responsible for spreading and controlling meth in that state. There is a plan to distribute meth, but it is ran by demonic influence. Another area that I see and hear a lot about is the twisting of the book of Revelations, about the different colored horses, matching up with the red and black in meth production. This is not what those scriptures are about.

79

The fifth theme they call somatic delusions. These folks are convinced that there is something very wrong with their bodies, that they omit foul odors, that they have bugs or flies crawling in or on their bodies. These people will avoid contact with society and often do more dope to make the symptoms continue in order to prove this to others. They will spend much time consulting doctors and taking tests to try and prove their imagined condition.

All of these conditions are very serious, especially to those who are being affected by them, the hallmark of these conditions are that these people will not listen to reason about their condition. I know I was in several of these categories, I thought I would never be free of this constant torment. These conditions are demonically driven and can be overcome with the Word of God!

You have to begin to take control of your thought life with the Word. Now while the scientific community will say that they don't know for sure if people with this kind of disorders are dangerous, I can tell you that without a shadow of doubt that people who are on meth with these different themes in operation in their lives are extremely dangerous to themselves and others around them. If there was any way to count the true suicide rate among meth users and other drugs, the numbers daily would be astounding!

I want to tell you about a dream the Lord game me shortly after my complete deliverance. First, I need to tell you that one of the main things I used to become paranoid about when I was on meth was that someone had been in my house or vehicle and dismantled it, hid something and then put it back together before I got home. This paranoia carried over, even after I was clean and delivered.

The dream started out as I was at the bottom of a stairway looking up. There was a certain board that looked like it had just been nailed back into place and had fresh caulking around it. I walked up to the board and ran my finger along the caulking, which came off like it had just been applied. I thought I had caught them this time. Then I looked around and it was demon spirits hovering about that were driving this into my mind. Then all of a sudden I was in a large room where there was a young boy that goes to our church and there was five or six of the creatures that looked semi-human but I knew they were demonic. All at once they pounced on this boy and were attacking him. All these demons had short swords and I had one also. I immediately grabbed a demon and threw it to the ground and physically was cutting its head off. After I cut its head off I looked up and there was my friend and pastor, Billy Ray Harvill. He was squatted down with his short sword, with a hoard of demons surrounding him. They were also squatted down and had their swords. He began speaking the Word to them and they started one by one driving the swords up under their chins into their heads, killing themselves.

Then I woke up. I thought about this for many days and the dream is still vivid in my imagination. The Holy Spirit revealed to me that it is the Word of God that is going to overcome and defeat the enemy. There is nothing we can do physically to combat a spiritual enemy. Hebrews 4:12 says, "For the Word of God is quick and powerful and sharper than any two edged sword, piercing even to the dividing asunder of Soul and Spirit and of the joints and marrow and is a discerner of the thoughts and intents of the heart. The word is quick and powerful and razor sharp in every direction and dimension." Remember it is your most powerful weapon and the most powerful thing that exists in the universe. Ephesians 6:12 says, "For we wrestle not against flesh and blood but against principalities, against powers, against the rulers of the darkness of this world, against spiritual wickedness in high places."

Horrors of Meth

I'd like to take this chapter and tell of some true and everyday stories of the kind of occurrences that go on in the meth world. I won't use names and let me say, since some of these cases might be pending that they are alleged. About a year and a half ago there was a pregnant mother with three small children who lived in a neighboring town. Her ex-boyfriend lived here, one night he decided to go up and kill this lady and her children. But he figured that he would need help, so he agreed to pay a couple a few hundred dollars worth of meth to help accomplish this. The story goes that these three people went to this girls house, the ex-boyfriend went to the door and convinced her to let him take her up to the store to get the kids some ice cream and groceries. While they were gone this couple entered the apartment and strangled the three children. They then waited for the man and pregnant girl to return from the store and then she was killed also. This is the thought process that is present in the majority of meth addicts.

Not too long ago, a story was in the paper of two men who decided to go arrowhead hunting while on meth, one of these men was also taking care of his two small children at the time. These kids were strapped in their carseats, it was the middle of summer with the windows rolled up. These men left them in the parked car, and proceeded to hunt arrowheads, when they returned they thought they had been gone 30 minutes. They soon realized that it had been eight hours, not 30 minutes the children were dead and had pulled their hair out as they suffocated.

Another newspaper tells of a man in California who entered a house, the parents had left for work. Upstairs sleeping were four or five children, ranging in age from six years old up to teenagers. One of the children woke up and looked downstairs, they saw a naked man barricading the door with furniture. He had a pitchfork. This man killed two of the children , stabbed a third. The survivors let themselves down out of a window and ran to the neighbors house and called the sheriff.

The next story comes from a psychologist friend of mine, who is co-sponsor of a weekly prayer/support group meeting. Her daughter and son-in-law were driving in a part of Kansas City, MO. They stopped at a stop light. Suddenly a man covered in blood jumped in their back seat and was screaming "they're after me they're going to kill me." He then proceeded to take off all of his clothes, fortunately they were able to console this man and take him to the emergency room. They found out he was tweaking on meth.

There are also multiple stories of people just overheating and dying. One of these was an area man who was laying naked in a motel parking lot, the police came there was a struggle and enroute to the police station this man collapsed and died. The reason I told this story was to get you to see a pattern among these stories. Why are many of these people naked when these things happen? My friend asked me about this and at first I just thought about this, then I went to the Word. In Luke 8:27-30 it says, "And when he went forth (Jesus) to land, there met him out the city a certain man, which had devils long time, and ware no clothes neither abode in any house, but in the tombs. When he saw Jesus, he cried out, and fell down before him, and with a loud voice said, what have I to do with thee, Jesus thou Son of God most high? I beseech thee, torment me not. (for he had commanded the unclean to come out of the man. For oftentimes it had caught him: and he was kept bound with chains and in fetters; and he brake the bands, and was driven into the wilderness.) And Jesus asked him, saying, What is thy name? And he said Legion: because many devils were entered into him." This is the reason people on meth and other drugs are doing these horrendous things, the sorcery of meth, crack, heroin etc. opens the gate of a person so that devils can enter.

Let's look at another newspaper story about a lady that was abducted by a boyfriend who then tied her up and proceeded to burn and torture her, poured acid on her. She was also sodomized and raped. Luckily he fell asleep at one point and she was able to escape. When the police came they found chemicals for a meth lab. Many stories in the paper tell of parents losing their parental rights after under the influence of meth they are having sex with their children and video taping it. Other parents are actually killing their own kids. I know for a fact that county jails all over our nation have stacks of the most perverted videos that were taken out of houses that are either cooking dope, selling or using.

Other stories of violence related with meth are many, for example one man cut his own childs head off after he was hallucinating that his child was a meth monster! Every time I pick up a paper and read of a bizarre killing, rape, suicide, abduction or something of this nature, I guarantee you 95% are meth related. The previous stories are just examples of how meth makes everyone who is on it think. There are no exceptions, once a person is on meth for any length of time this is how they begin to think, these are the kinds of things they dwell on. What I am telling you is the truth about meth, everyday I get letters from prisoners who would testify that these are the truths of the meth world.

What's Cookin' In Your Neighborhood?

This chapter will give people a tool to see what's going on in their neighborhood. A lot of people know that a loved one is caught in something, but don't have the knowledge of what to look for. If you think you're living next to a meth lab here are some indicators:

- Unusual, strong odors that might resemble urine, solvents, ammonia, ether, acetone or chemical smells.
- Lots of traffic, especially at night; people coming and going at unusual times.
- An extra effort to cover their windows, they might also try to reinforce doors.
- Vehicles could be loaded with trunk-like containers or large duffel bags, any chemistry glassware, tubing, containers of acid or any type of solvent.
- Residents might never put their trash out, or always burn trash
- Folks might be smoking outside because of fumes or they might have their windows open at unusual times of the year.
- Any clear glass jugs or containers with duct tape on them.
- Yards will usually be trashy and unkempt, but not always.
- Lots of vehicles that are being traded for dope and/or unfinished projects.

The following is a list of some of the chemicals and ingredients that would indicate meth production:
- acetone
- camp stove fuel, Coleman fuel

- toluene
- ether or starting fluids
- propane tanks for anhydrous ammonia
- mineral spirits
- lithium batteries or graphite
- sulfuric acid
- hydrochloric acid
- Heet
- 7% iodine solution
- hydrogen peroxide
- Red Devil Lye
- rock, Epsom and table salt
- red phosphorous
- iodine crystals
- match books
- rubbing alcohol
- mini thins or cold tablets
- hot plates
- gun blue

These are just a few of the most common things to look for. The list is actually much longer. If you find quantities of any of these items, it is a good indicator of meth production. There will also be containers of liquids that have separated levels within the container. Another container might have a white sludge in it which is pill waste. Coffee filters with this white sludge or a coffee filters with a reddish brown substance.

The following are signs to look for if you suspect that someone is on meth:

- paranoia
- drastic mood swings
- down right mean
- hallucinations audio and visual
- severe depression
- memory loss

- drastic weight loss
- acne, sores
- aggressive or violent behavior
- very dark circles under eyes
- suspicious
- large pupils
- unusual or perverted sexual requests
- always looking out the window
- false sense of confidence
- emotions blunted
- impaired speech
- not sleeping
- not eating
- anxious or fidgety
- priorities out of order
- neglect of fatherly and motherly instincts
- neglected personal hygiene
- neglecting house work
- a grad plot against them

Again this is just a list of some of the indicators.

The Arena

About three years ago, I had a dream. I was sitting in an arena. It was huge. It was larger than Arrowhead Stadium in Kansas City, MO. This arena was full and more and more people were continuously flooding in. I was sitting about halfway up in the stands watching everything that was going. It was absolutely crazy in there. My wife was sitting on my left and this old man was sitting on my right. Around us were groups of people of different ages, each in their own little group. One group was dragging a guy and beating him to death. Out of this same group this mans wife watched as she fixed up on more dope. Another group was molesting children, others watched and filmed it. Other groups were sitting in there, that resembled youth in the Gothic style of dress, but all of these groups were in common.

There were demons and demonic activity all around. This arena was packed and more people were flooding in continuously. The best way that I could describe it was, imagine the most bizarre rapes, abductions, murders, suicides, pornographic acts and abominations that could be performed by humans that is what was going in this arena. This arena is the world of methamphetamine. After a while we were just sitting there watching all of this demonic activity, then this old man turned to me and snarled that Phyllis Jackson. This was a lady in our church who had been praying for me. I got up and took my wife's hand and we walked out of this arena and didn't look back. I woke up and thought, man that was a strange dream. I did think about this for a couple of years, then the Holy Spirit brought it back to my remembrance.

What I want to portray to you the meth user is that this is what you are a part of. You may say that I'm not involved with these kind of things, wrong if you're not there yet, just wait. These things that I described are what await every addict. Let me give you an example, let's say that you cook a batch of meth and you front so and so a half an ounce and then someone else gets an eightball and on down the line until maybe the last guy only gets a quarter gram. But this guy who gets the quarter gram has already been up for two weeks and is tweaked out of his head and kills himself or someone else, or maybe that night they rape their step daughter. This scenario could go on and on.

What I want to say is that you can walk out of the world of meth and be victorious. You can get your life back and you can learn how to kick the devil in the teeth. These things don't happen overnight, but if you decide to serve the Lord, you will be very glad you did. Understand that God is calling you. Ephesians 2:1-8 says, "And you hath he quickened who were dead in trespasses and sins; Wherein in time past ye walked according to the course of this world, according to the prince of the power of the air, the spirit that now worketh in the children of disobedience; Among whom also we all had our conversation in times past in the lusts of our flesh, fulfilling the desires of the flesh and of the mind; and were by nature the children of wrath, even as others. But God who is rich in mercy, for his great love wherewith he loved us, Even we were dead in sin, hath quickened us together with Christ, (by grace ye are saved;) and hath raised us up together in heavenly places in Christ Jesus: that in the ages to come he might show the exceeding riches of his grace in his kindness toward us through Christ Jesus. For by grace are ye saved through faith; and that not of yourselves; it is the gift of God.

Something For Everyone

What I want to do in this chapter is share something that the Lord showed me out of the Word. I'll start off, by painting a picture for you. Imagine a masterpiece, some picture that by the world's standards would be called a masterpiece. Maybe the Mona Lisa, or some picture by Rembrandt, or possibly Michaelangelo. Imagine the intricate layers of color and the time it took to produce such a work of art. John 10:10 says, "The thief cometh not, but for to steal, kill and destroy:" God has a name for the drug world and especially meth production, it is called sorcery. Meth production in our society is Satan's masterpiece, whether you're in Asia and you call it *yaba*, or you're in Hawaii it's *batu*, or here in good ol America it goes by crank, speed, or many other names. People ask me what makes this drug different? When everyone whoever tries meth begins, a weave of deceit is begun that is tailor made just for them. This deceit is woven throughout their life until they reach a point where them and their family can be killed, stole from and finally destroyed. A hook called envy will be put into you that will begin to guide your every step. Proverbs 27:4 says, "Wrath is cruel, and anger is outrageous; but who is able to stand before envy?"

Let's go to the book of Acts 13:9. Paul is on his first missionary journey and he is dealing with a sorcerer. "Then Saul, (who also is called Paul) filled with the Holy Ghost, set his eyes on him." Let's stop here and look at this first part Paul here is filled with the Holy Ghost, So we need to pay careful attention to what is said in verse 10. "O full of all subtility and all mischief, thou child of the devil, thou enemy of all righteousness, wilt thou not cease to pervert the right ways of the Lord?" Everyone who is a student of the Word of God needs to pay close attention to what was just said here in verse 10. Nowhere else in the entire Bible is anything dealt with as harshly as sorcery. Let's look at the first statement in verse 10, O full of all subtility. Subtility means closely woven, ingenious, intricate, discriminating, hard to solve, crafty, wily, sly. In the garden in Genesis 3 verse 1 says, "Now the serpent was more subtle than any beast of the field which the Lord God had made." In Genesis the serpent was more subtle, but in Acts 13 sorcery is filled with all subtility. Pay attention no where else in the Bible is anything said to be filled with all subtility. If we go on in verse 13 it says that sorcery is filled with all mischief, one definition of mischief is to cause harm or damage. Verse 13 goes on to say thou child of the devil, now that is one strong statement. If you are a child of the devil, then you must have an inheritance. The devil and his angels have an inheritance and it's called the lake of fire. Matthew 25:41 says, "Then shall he say also unto them on the left hand, Depart from me, ye cursed, into everlasting fire, prepared for the devil and his angels."

Let's go on in verse 10. It then says, "Thou enemy of all righteousness", an enemy is a person who hates another and wishes to injure him; also one hostile to another a soldier, citizen of a hostile nation. If you are involved with the meth world, you are a soldier for the devil. Verse 10 then says, "Wilt thou not cease to pervert the right ways of the Lord?" Pervert is a perfect word for the drug world. Listen closely if you or your loved one is still involved in this world of subtility, mischief, a child of the devil, an enemy of righteousness, that is perverting the right ways of the Lord, What do you do? Through the leading of the Holy Ghost you should do whatever it takes to come against this evil that is encompassing our land. Whatever it takes, whatever it takes, whatever it takes. Through this book, I have tried to encourage and tell the truth about the meth world. Now it is up to you on what you will do to come against this in your town and in your family. Romans 12:21 says, "Be not overcome of evil, but overcome evil with good." I see and hear everyday firsthand the destruction that is taking place. People get into their own little world of comfort and do not want to address this subject, wake up America and the world.

The King of Terrors

When was the last time you were afraid? No I mean scared to death, terrified, unable to move, hiding for hours on end waiting to be killed? Some might say well I've never experienced that. I need you to really think about this with me. A fear that turns into terror, the definition of terror is 1) an intense overpowering fear 2) One that instills intense fear 3) Violence committed especially by a group for political purposes. Let's look at the first definition, intense overpowering fear, this means a superior force that is overcoming, overwhelming would be a better word. Now imagine you're in your own house and you are being overwhelmed. Stop, and please think about this for a moment. A fear mixed in with familiar voices, talking to you, shapes and demons appearing. Swat teams outside your house and a dead body that is laying in the living room. Voices so many voices turning your wife or girlfriend into the whore. Smells and stains appearing before your eyes, a definite plan unfolding with a very intelligent, masterful voice leading to some sort of imminent destruction. Fear that is so overpowering, images that fit into the plan of this voice. The voice sounds like your own.

The plot is to kill you and even your closest families members are in on it. This intense fear begins to pull triggers in your mind and possibly the trigger of the 12 gauge that you are gripping in your hands. Job 18:10-12, 14 says, "The snare is laid for him in the ground, and a trap for him in the way. Terrors shall make him afraid on every side, and shall drive him to his feet. His confidence shall be rooted out of his tabernacle, (house) and it shall bring him to the king of terrors." A terror that dwells where you live and the door to that terror is methamphetamine!

The second definition is one that instills intense fear, one, who is that one in this case? The third definition violence, committed by a group for political reasons, now we are getting somewhere. There is a group out there called one third of the fallen angels and whatever other spirits go along with them, and they have a leader named Satan, who has found a tool of destruction unlike anything before, something that is made without fear, but full of fear at the same time. The plot originally was to overthrow the kingdom of God, in Isaiah 14:13-16 "For thou hast said in thine heart, I (Lucifer) will ascend into heaven, I will exalt my throne above the stars of God: I will sit also upon the mount of the congregation, in the sides of the north: I will ascend above the heights of the clouds; I will be like the most High. That was the plan according to Satan. Yet thou shalt be brought down to hell, to the sides of the pit. They that see thee shall narrowly look upon thee and consider thee, saying Is this the man that made the earth to tremble, that did shake the kingdoms:" Revelation 20:1-3 says "And I saw as angel come down from heaven, having the key of the bottomless pit and a great chain in his hand. And he laid hold on the dragon, that old serpent, which is the Devil and Satan and bound him a thousand years. And cast him into the bottomless pit and shut him up and set a seal upon him, that he should deceive the nations no more, till the thousand years should be fulfilled and after that he must be loosed for a little season." Time is shortening, and the signs are clear.

The Deadly Mixture

There is a mixture out there that escalates the power of meth to an even higher level. It is being taught all across this land, in our prisons, in our children's movies, in games, comics, television and everywhere you look. Those that practice the art of witchcraft, might be very offended at this chapter. But I'm talking to those of you who know what I'm talking about. When you involve meth with people who are practicing satanism and witchcraft, you get a whole new level of demonic manifestation and demonic activity. When I was strung on dope, I came across a few people who fit this category and I can tell you they know what they are doing to people with the assistance of spirits. The crossing over into the spiritual realm happens frequently. Guard your family and teach them well.

The Sacrifice

Psalm 106:36-39 says, "And they served their idols (methamphetamine) which were a snare onto them. Yea, they sacrificed their sons and their daughters unto devils. And shed innocent blood, even the blood of their daughters, whom they sacrificed onto the idols of Canaan: and the land was polluted with blood. Thus were they defiled with their own works and went a whoring with their own inventions."

The definition of sacrifice out of the dictionary is 1) an offering, as of a life or object, to a deity. 2) a giving up of one thing for the sake of another. 3) a loss incurred in selling. All over this world right now, parents are sacrificing their children to the demonic gods of methamphetamine, which in fact aren't gods at all, but only fallen angels who will soon be thrown into the lake of fire. Give up these precious lives to a bag of white powder. Selling them into pornography, and filming it when at the heart of it is meth. Mothers wanting meth more than their children. Parents who are teaching their own children to use and whore their lives away to meth. Your every move being controlled by some demon. The slaughter of families, being slaughtered by their own parents hands.

This word sacrifice from Psalm 106:37 comes from the word *Zabach* which means to slaughter, kill, sacrifice. This verb is used primarily to describe the killing of animals, even idolatrous sacrifices. This word means private individuals who brought sacrifices at their own expense. I pray in the Name of Jesus, that those of you who have children will turn from this sacrificing of your children to meth and serve the living God Jesus Christ, who will soon be returning, amen.

The ultimate sacrifice was made when the Lord God, maker of heaven and earth sent His Son Jesus Christ to die for our sins, that through him we may have eternal life. When you become a servant of meth, guess who's children are going to be sacrificed to satan? Yours. And you'll be the one who does the sacrificing.

Today as I was getting ready to write this chapter, I stood up from my computer and walked over to a window that looks into my back yard. There in the yard were two of my daughters. One was digging in a sand box and the other was riding her bike, they were laughing and playing. The sun was shining down on them and the birds were chirping. I praised the Lord for my new life in Him.

Section 2

Winning the War

Psalm 144:1 says, "BLESSED be the Lord my strength, which teacheth my hands to war and my fingers to fight;" How serious are the times that we are living in? How important is your family to you? The war is on and we need to be aware of the stakes. What's riding on these few years that you and I have left. Think about that one. I believe that the Lord wants us to understand, and to know without a shadow of doubt that we are the mouthpiece of God. That we are a part of a divine plan and I believe that the number one obligation that we have is to our family.

So this section of the book will be full of short chapters, that will be devoted to ways that we can wage and effective war against the enemy. Ways that through the Word of God we can gain back everything that we have lost. Effective prayers that work, knowing above all else that the Word is alive and well. The Word of God works in every situation. That by staying around the things of God that you can have a powerful spirit led life full of victory. Matthew 16:26 says "For what is a man profited, if he shall gain the whole world, and lose his own soul? of what shall a man give in exchange for his soul?"

My good friend and writing partner Bill Harvill preached a sermon once that used the preceding scripture and the Holy Ghost said to him say it like this. What does it profit a man to gain the whole world and to lose his very own? Sometimes it's very easy to get caught up in everything else besides your family. Especially if you get involved in ministry work. The devil is very good at what he does and one of the biggest ways that he fights against you, is a very subtle attack of distractions that will keep you from spending the quality time that your family needs.

The number one ministry that you will ever have is to your family. Let me repeat that. The number one ministry that you will ever have is your family. One time I was talking with my mother in law and she told me that "Steve, sure the devil would like to kill you, but who he really wants is Daella and your kids." When one of my kids has a ball game I am there, even if I have to skip a regularly scheduled meeting. The Holy Ghost can get the job done with a friend of mine filling in for me that night. Praise God! How far are you willing to go, to make sure that your family makes it? Have you already given up on them? Now Faith, Now Faith, Now Faith in the Word of God. We will begin with Faith, a relationship with faith. Hebrews 11:6 says, "But without faith it is impossible to please him: for he that cometh to God must believe that he is and that he is a rewarder of them that diligently seek him."

Faith Has The Power

Where are you at? What is it that you believe? What doctrine are you caught up in? Are you willing to change? If what you believe wasn't correct would you want to know?

First John 2:27 says, "But the anointing which ye have received of him abideth in you, and ye need not that any man teach you: but as the same anointing teacheth you of all things and is truth and is no lie, and even as it hath taught you, ye shall abide in him."

You might say, "What does the preceding scripture have to do with faith?" God is wanting to do something with your life that only He can do. I want to encourage you to focus on reading the Word of God. I rarely read any other book. There is an anointing to go along with whatever it is that the Lord wants to accomplish in your life. So what I want to encourage you to do, is to let the Holy Spirit be your number one teacher, not some book or even this book. This book is only a guideline.

Romans 10:17 says, "So then faith cometh by hearing and hearing by the word of God." Listen closely. The only way that a person is going to have faith and be an overcomer, is to put themselves in a place several times a week to hear the Word of God.

When I first started to try and come off of meth, we had just moved down to the country and started attending Shoal Creek Revival Church. I was actually stuck schizophrenic, most of the time. Even though I hadn't been doing any meth for a while, my mind would continue to be paranoid, just like I had been doing dope. Well for the next year and a half, I attended church several times a week and would drink a 12 pack of beer every night and smoke a couple of joints, but I was continually hearing the Word of God on a regular basis. And changes in me were gradually taking place. I opened the door wide open to meth again at the end of that year and it took over quickly and tried to destroy my family once again.

The Word of God does not fall void. All those times I had been hearing the Word, along with prayers and God's plan I was set free from meth. Faith cometh by hearing and hearing by the Word of God. This battle that you are in can be overcome and the Word of God will win in your life, if you will let it. No matter what you are going through, not under any circumstances, never stop going to church. If you do not love your church, you're in the wrong one. There is a definition out of the dictionary for faith that I really like, and it is, faith equals absolute certainty in the trustworthiness of another, belief, trust, confidence and reliance. Absolute certainty in God, His son Jesus, The Holy Ghost and the Word of God! You can count on God and His Word. Man may have let you down in this world, maybe even someone in the church community, but not God and his Word, they will never let you down. This is what real faith is all about, knowing, being assured, absolute certainty that your faith in the Lord and His Word is the real thing and the only true way to go.

Hebrews 11:1 says, "Now faith is the substance of things hoped for, the evidence of things not seen." Is there anything in your life that you are hoping for? Would you like to see your family back together? Or maybe a loved one delivered from meth? Maybe you'd just like to have your mind back. One of the first things that I asked the Lord for was, that if I could just not be schizophrenic. I would be a very grateful and a happy man. I found that by standing on God's Word, I was eventually completely delivered from paranoia and fear. It didn't happen overnight, it took over two years for this to happen. I thank God for this.

James 1:3, 4 says, "Knowing this, that the trying of your faith worketh patience. Patience is a great lesson to learn and one that must be learned by someone that is overcoming a meth addiction. But let patience have her perfect work, that ye may be perfect and entire, wanting nothing." Complete, whole, restored, having a faith that no matter what the circumstances and what you're facing that

God will see you through. Right now the things that you are going through are a lesson that you are being taught and will prove to be valuable later. Know this that if God is for us who can be against us. We are in a battle and sometimes the going gets tough, you might feel unworthy and weak and unable to live up to the so-called Christian standards.

Most the time this is a religious spirit trying to work on you and others around you. You shall know them by their fruits and what comes out of their mouth. Be wise as a serpent and harmless as a dove. When another Christian lets you down, usually God is trying to teach you something. Don't put any man on a pedestal, he will let you down. Only Jesus is to be put on a pedestal.

Hebrews 11:6 says, "But without faith it is impossible to please him: for he that cometh to God must believe that he is, and that he is a rewarder of them that diligently seek him." Rewards can be sweet and diligently seeking him is a life long project, where there is always more to learn. There is a difference between being a believer and becoming a disciple. John 8:31 says, "Then said Jesus to those Jews which believed on him, If ye continue in my word, then are ye my disciples indeed." I hear this statement all the time, "I don't have to go to church to be a Christian" that statement is true, but if you are going to overcome drug addiction, or help someone who's addicted, you must become a disciple. Continue on, stand fast and have faith in the Word of God!

107

Some Things Only God Can Do

Luke 18:27 says, "And he said The things which are impossible with men are possible with God." Luke 1:37 says, "For with God nothing shall be impossible." Everyday I receive letters and often times during the week I get to talk to someone who is still being run by meth and a pack of devils. I get to visit with parents who have tried everything and usually given up hope. And the letters are filled with testimonies that seem like only an act of God could heal this situation. I don't claim to know much, but I do believe we have a sovereign God who can do anything he wants and a God who will back up his Word. The Scriptures are full of promises of deliverance to his people.

Hebrews 13:8 says, "Jesus Christ the same yesterday, and today and forever." I know what he's done for one he'll do for another. What is you situation? Are you a parent who really would like to help your son or daughter, but your life is full of sin and you don't really know who God is yourself? Where is your relationship with Him? Have you cried out in repentance before him over your own life? Have you truly accepted Jesus and his Word? Are you playing church? The reason I'm saying these things to you, are so that if you do decide to ask for the Lord's help, you need to be right with him also. He knows that we need his help, and I know it took an act from God to deliver me.

Remember when earlier we were talking about faith. I know if I pray according to His Word and ask in faith for a loved one on meth. That we serve a family oriented all powerful God, who is interested in His family. A God who will bring that person to a place of choice in their own lives and he is capable of bringing home those lost loved ones who at one time knew and served him. Some great scriptures that you can stand on are Job 5:8-11. "I would seek onto God and unto God would I commit my cause: Which doeth great things and unsearchable; marvellous things without number. Who giveth rain upon the earth and sendeth waters upon the fields: To set up on high those that be low; that those which mourn may be exalted to safety."

Many times in my own life when I pray, the Lord will then show me how the thing that I prayed for can be accomplished and will actually give me the ideas that I need to make it happen. Many people will pray and just expect some magic wand to be waved and fix a problem. What I'm saying is that many times when you pray, God will lead you in a direction that he will show you to help that person. Don't ever give up. I can remember over two years ago praying for a friend of mine, and this guy seemed like an impossible case, time went by and eventually he ended up in jail where he accepted the Lord. Since then he's out and things have not been exactly perfect, but I know God has a plan for his life and is working things out in him, just like he is me. Some things only God can do, his word is all powerful.

The following are some prayers out of the Word of God, that we have seen results from and have had testimonies from people of these occurrences taking place. The preceding scripture in this chapter was Job 5:8 is a place that you can seek God over your situation and commit your cause to Him. Now going further in the same chapter of Job 5:12 says, "He disappointeth the devices of the crafty, so that their hands cannot perform their enterprise." We have stood in agreement, using this scripture that the hands that are cooking meth would not be able to perform their enterprise. After praying this we have had reports and testimonies of batches of dope not turning out.

I encourage everyone who reads this book to mix a little faith with this scripture and pray it over anyone that you know of that cooks dope, including loved ones. Also please pray this in agreement over the worldwide drug lords and their cooks, that God would disappoint the devices of the crafty so that their hand cannot perform their enterprise in the Name of Jesus! Pray this prayer continually!

Job 5 continues on in verse 13, 14 saying, "He taketh the wise in their own craftiness; and the counsel of the froward is carried headlong. What will begin to happen to them, saying they meet with darkness in the daytime, and grope in the noonday as in the night." What will happen through these prayers is that God will begin to work the people that need delivered into a place of being sobered up, usually it's in jail. The Holy Spirit comes to the jails and to the dope houses and the meth labs and begins speaking to these men and women. It's through your prayers that the deliverance will begin to take place.

Many times it is when man is at his lowest point in life, when he or she will begin to start looking for answers. There are many, that when they find out that they are involved with, sorcery, and that the devil is controlling them, will turn from the meth world and come into the light of Jesus Christ. John 8:12 says, "Then spake Jesus again unto them saying, I am the light of the world, he that followeth me shall not walk in darkness, but shall have the light of life."

Another place in the word is in Acts 13 Paul is on his first missionary journey and is trying to lead a man named Sergius Paulus to the faith, but there was a certain sorcerer who withstood him and sought to turn the deputy from the faith. Maybe you have someone that you are wanting to reach with the Gospel, but there is a certain sorcerer that is withstanding you or a loved one. Look at how Paul addresses this man in verse 10. "And said, O full of all subtility and all mischief, thou child of the devil, thou enemy of all righteousness, wilt thou not cease to pervert the right ways of the Lord?" And look what Paul says in verse 11, "And now, behold the hand of the Lord is upon thee, and thou shalt be blind, not seeing the sun for a season, And immediately there fell on him a mist and a darkness, and he went about seeking some to lead him by the hand." Call out that person's name who is practicing sorcery and say in the Name of Jesus and now behold, the hand of the Lord is upon you, and you shalt be blind, not seeing the sun for a season, and immediately a mist and darkness will fall upon you and you will go about seeking some to lead you by the hand. This word darkness is actually *Skotos* it means to restrain, stop, for when we are overcome by the night we are forced to stop. After this was stated to this sorcerer in Acts 13:12 says, "Then the deputy, when he saw what was done, believed, being astonished at the doctrine of the Lord." Have faith in what God's Word says because some things only God can do and he will do them through His Word!

Spiritual Warfare

When you look at the life of Jesus, He did many things. He addressed everything that we ourselves will have to face. He is always addressing us with His Word. He lived life with His disciples, ate, drank and visited with sinners, who were in need of a savior. He addressed the religious groups of the day and the religious people who thought that they were speaking for Him. In reality they didn't even know Him. When I got involved with this ministry, I didn't know that there were so many lesson to learn and that it can get complicated very quickly.

I believe that God is a god of simplicity and that His methods and motives are simple and clear cut. He deals with each of us as individuals and will teach you through His Word. That many times it is easy to get off track and to focus on only one part of ministry, when in reality our entire life is a journey and we get to decide what direction it will go. Aren't you thankful that we have a God, that through His Son Jesus Christ and through the working of the Holy Ghost, we have a blessed assurance of eternal life! That we have a road map of His life that can teach us everything that we need to know. And on that road that Jesus traveled, he and his disciples often ran into the devil.

Believer or Disciple?

Acts 5:14 says, "And believers were the more added to the Lord, multitudes both of men and women." This word believers comes from the word *Pisteuo* or *Pistis,* which means faith, belief, to believe, to have a mental persuasion, to believe in or on Jesus Christ, an implying knowledge or assent to and confidence in him, being persuaded. In general it implies, a knowledge of and confidence in certain divine truths, especially those of the Gospel, as it produces good works.

In the Gospel of Luke 10:2 says, "Therefore said he unto them, the harvest truly is great, but the labourers are few: pray ye therefore the Lord of the harvest, that he would send forth labourers into His harvest." Right now many believe that the harvest is in full force, and I believe this also. The harvest truly is so great and there are many believers being added to His church daily. What I want to do is encourage you to go past being only a believer and strive to be a disciple! Let's pray together that the Lord of the harvest would send forth laborers (disciples) in the name of Jesus.

Many times people are misled because they have simply a knowledge and accept basic religious truths without good works and therefore have false faith! Many are caught up in being religious, thinking that not smoking, drinking or cussing makes them a Christian. They are whispered to by a religious spirit and their own righteousness and never reach out to help others. They want to condemn others and point their finger.

James 2:17-20 says, "Even so faith, if it hath not works is dead, being alone. Yea a man may say, Thou hast faith, and I have works: shew me thy faith without thy works and I will shew thee my faith by my works. Thou believest that there is one God; thou doest well: the devils also believe and tremble. But wilt thou know, O vain man, that faith without works is dead?"

"Then said Jesus to those Jews which believed on him, If ye continue in my word, then are ye my disciples indeed; And ye shall know the truth and the truth shall make you free" (John 8:31, 32).

I am a firm believer that there is a difference between believers and disciples and that we all should strive to become a disciple. Also if you are going to overcome a drug addiction, you must become a disciple! If you are wanting to help your loved ones, who are caught in the meth world, you yourself should strive to become a disciple and labourer!

The word disciple comes from the word *Mathetas* and it means to learn, it means more than a mere pupil or learner, one who adheres and accepts instruction given to him or her and make it a rule of conduct. To teach and exercise power in performing miracles and tasks through the help of His (Jesus and Holy Ghost's) authority and power transferred to them. To learn by putting what one learns to experience.

Power Given

"And when he had called unto him his twelve disciples, he gave them power against unclean spirits, to cast them out, and to heal all manner of sickness and all manner of disease" (Matthew 10:1).

"And he called unto him the twelve, and began to send them forth by two and two; and gave the power over unclean spirits" (Mark 6:7).

"Then he called his twelve disciples together, and gave them power and authority over all devils, and to cure diseases. And he sent them to preach the Kingdom of God, and to heal the sick" (Luke 9:1, 2).

"After these things the Lord appointed other seventy also, and sent them two and two before his face into every city and place, whither he himself would come" (Luke 10:1).

"And the seventy returned again with joy, saying, Lord even the devils are subject unto us through thy name" (Luke 10:17).

Who was the power over unclean spirits given to? His disciples. Let me say that again, Who was the power over unclean spirits given to? His disciples.

The reason that I am first establishing this difference between believers and disciples is because, there is much confusion among the Christian world, concerning this subject of Spiritual Warfare, and I myself have been caught up in it.

Again John 8:31 says, ". . . If ye continue in my word, then are ye my disciples indeed;" It doesn't say if you continue in every other function, that you are His disciple—in His word! Are you His disciple? Are you willing to do the things that he commanded? "And these signs shall follow them that believe; In my name shall they cast out devils;" (Mark 16:17).

116

An Exact Match

As we continue with this subject of spiritual warfare, let me tell you about an exact match. And that match is the similarities between people in the Bible who are being demonically afflicted and those that are on methamphetamine! In Matthew 8:28-34, Luke 8:26-39 and Mark 5:1-19, Jesus is dealing with a demon possessed individual and in the account out of Matthew there were two individuals. This is what the Bible says about the condition of them. They lived and dwelled in the tombs. I like to make this comparison with the living conditions of the households of those that are on meth. The windows are covered, letting no light in, trash everywhere, piles of clothes, pornography, furniture tore up and just the overall atmosphere is the dwelling place of the devil. It also says in these three accounts that no man could tame him, that they cried out, cutting themselves, wore no clothes, that they would break the bonds and chains asunder, that they were driven of the devil into the wilderness. This phrase was driven translates from the word *elauno* which means to push as oars or demonic power, to carry, drive, row.

In Mark 9 Jesus was dealing with a devil that his disciples couldn't cast out. Verse 18 says "And wheresoever he taketh him, he teareth him; and he foameth, and gnasheth with him teeth, and pineth away: and I spake to thy disciples that they should cast him out; and they could not."

In this preceding scripture it says that the devil taketh him. This word taketh comes from the root word *Ktalambano* which means "to take, to seize, to lay hold of, to apprehend." It means that the darkness did not admit or receive the light. The darkness is here presented as being so thick that the light could not penetrate it. It also means to come upon and to overtake.

The other phrase that I want to look at in Mark 9:18 says and gnasheth with his teeth. The word gnasheth comes from the Greek word *trizo*, which means to grate teeth in a frenzy, to gnash. Everyone who is on meth grinds their teeth—everyone! Let's look a little further in Mark 9:22. "And often times it hath cast him into the fire, and into the waters, to destroy him: but if thou canst do anything, have compassion on us, and help us." We are in need of Jesus' help everyday. I promise you the world of meth is the most demonic, devil ridden area of our society and it is spreading rapidly.

These are only a few examples out of Scripture of how those that are being demonically controlled will act. In Mark 9:18 the disciples could not cast this one out. In verse 19 Jesus says "bring him unto me." I encourage you to bring the loved ones who needs deliverance to the throne of Jesus in intercessory prayer to have others stand in agreement with you over your loved ones life. "Jesus said unto him, If thou canst believe, all things are possible to him that believeth" (Mark 9:23). Some things only God can do but it's our job to do everything that the Holy Spirit leads us to do.

In Mark 9:29 Jesus said to them "This kind can come forth by nothing but by prayer and fasting." I encourage to pray and fast for the loved one that you are wanting the Lord to reach. Jesus said in Luke 11:20 "But if I with the finger of God cast out devils, no doubt the kingdom of God is come upon you."

Casting Them Out

I want to keep this chapter as simple as possible. These are some of the simple facts that I have learned about this subject of casting out demons. First know this, it's not you casting them out. The Holy Ghost will do the work. God's holy Word will do the Work. There is no need for fear. God will use you to speak His word with authority and He will supply the power to get the job done. I want you to read the following scripture again. "But the anointing which ye have received of him abideth in you, and ye need not that any man teach you: but as the same anointing teacheth you of all things, and is truth, and is no lie, and even as it hath taught you, ye shall abide in him" (1 John 2:27). God will teach you, however, the following are just some basics that I have learned.

1) The Holy Ghost will reveal to you the time and what demon to cast out. The Holy Ghost will also empower you for this. Jesus always sent his disciples out two by two and I believe you should always have a strong brother or sister in Christ accompany you when doing this kind of work.

2) Does the person want this thing out of them? If they do, first make sure that they are born again and have made Jesus Lord. Have them confess out loud in the Name of Jesus that they want all evil spirits out of them. This will depend a lot on them. I have seen people who wanted the devil gone and others who didn't. Don't cast it out unless they want it gone and are willing to fill their life with the things of God. Because the Bible says that this evil spirit will try and return and bring seven more, more wicked than itself. See Luke 11:26.

3) Remember not everyone is demon possessed, many are only oppressed. I have found those that have a devil inside of them are

120

usually in torment and the Holy Spirit will reveal these things to you. They eyes, I have found to be one of the best indicators. Many times they're almost like a glaze and they won't want to look you in the eye for very long. Also that thing inside of them will start getting nervous when it knows that you are going to cast it out. Don't be surprised if it grunts or growls at you and may even talk to you and try and intimidate you. Remember Jesus has the keys and all power and authority has been given to Him.

4) Mark 16:17 says, "And these signs shall follow them that believe; In my name shall they cast out devils. . . ." Use Jesus' word and the words that he used when He cast out demons. In Mark 9 say (name of evil spirit) I charge thee, come out of him or her and enter no more into him. IN THE NAME OF JESUS, again have the person confess and command out loud in the Name of Jesus that they want these Spirits out of them. You need to study the words that Jesus used for yourself and familiarize yourself.

5) Remember this many people after the demons are gone might still feel afflicted and not completely healed. Let me tell you a little story. My family has rental properties and many times after the tenants who had trashed the house were gone, we had to come in and begin cleaning up and sometimes it required major repairs. The damage had been done and it was a matter of time and using the right tools to put that house back together again. Tell them not to get discouraged, that the healing process may take some time, that after the demonic tenants leave their house, it will take being around the Word of God. Sometimes it may take a while for complete recovery.

6) Listen to these words out of Matthew 12:43, 44: "When the unclean spirit is gone out of a man, he walketh through dry places, seeking rest, and findeth none. Then he saith, I will return into my house from whence I came out; and when he is come, he findeth it empty, swept and garnished." The key word here is empty. Explain to the person that they should seek the baptism of the Holy Ghost (speaking in tongues) to help fill this emptiness and should pray in tongues every time they are tempted to return to their old life-style.

7) Tell them to anoint their house with oil, every doorway and

window, and command that no unclean spirit can stay there in the name of the Father, Son and Holy Ghost. Also sometimes a good housecleaning is required, getting rid of certain items that are not of God.

Warning: Do not get out of balance in this area. The ministry does not revolve around casting out demons. Many people get totally out of balance in this area. Jesus said in Matthew 7:21-23, "Not every one that saith unto me Lord, Lord, shall enter into the kingdom of heaven; but he that doeth the will of my Father which is in heaven. Many will say to me in that day, Lord, Lord, have we not prophesied in thy Name? and in thy name cast out devils? and in thy name done many wonderful works? And then will I profess unto them, I never knew you: depart from me, ye that work iniquity." We overcome evil with good. Verse 22, I believe deals with three types of false ministry in the body of Christ.

Blasphemy

Matthew 12:31 says, "Wherefore I say unto you, All manner of sin and blasphemy shall be forgiven unto men: but the blasphemy against the Holy Ghost shall not be forgiven unto men. And Whosoever speaketh a word against the Son of man, it shall be forgiven him: but whosoever speaketh against the Holy Ghost, it shall not be forgiven him, neither in this world, neither in the world to come."

Everyone that reads this book should know this, that satanism and witchcraft is alive and well in the world of methamphetamine. There are many who practice incantations and spells. I can even trace, through letters, one of the first meth cooks that came into our area, and taught people to cook dope was in fact a satanist and would cast spells over his dope.

Understand that methamphetamine and its production is part of a great satanic plan. Many of these people know what blasphemy of the Holy Ghost is and are required to commit this act of high treason. I myself, back when I was on meth was hanging out with a man who was involved with the occult. One night, out of the blue, he took out a Bible and turned to the preceding scripture about blaspheming the Holy Ghost and proceeded to read out loud this scripture and began to cuss out the Holy Ghost and dared him to try and throw him into hell. Even with myself being under the influence of methamphetamine, it was one of the most awful things that I have ever witnessed. You wouldn't believe the darkness and evil this brought in over the next few days. I even wanted to kill this man myself. Be wise there are enemies of the cross out there who will disguise themselves. But in reality there is no hope for them. Philippians 3:18 says, "For many walk, of whom I have told you often, and now tell you even weeping,

124

that they are the enemies of the cross of Christ."

Becoming Addicted Again

First Corinthians 16:15 says, "I beseech you, brethren, (ye know the house of Stephanas, that it is the first fruits of Achaia, and that they have addicted themselves to the ministry of the saints,)" This is the only place in the Bible that the word addicted is used. And what is it that we are to become addicted to? The Word says the ministry of the saints. Well the first saints in my life are my family, my wife, children and parents. This is the place the most damage has been done because of our addiction to meth. What I want to do is to be continually changing, continually improving. This is a life long process, a true work of patience. Hebrew 6:12 says "That ye be not slothful, but followers of them who through faith and patience inherit the promises." Faith in His Word, mixed in with a big batch of patience you will inherit the promises. Amen Glory to Jesus.

First Things First

Praise the Lord! In everything give thanks to our Creator! Remember, first things first everyday. Every day is the first day of our new life. Starting off the day in an attitude of praise, thankfulness, and praying for people you don't like is a good way to begin each day. Every one is looking for what the will of the Father is in their individual life. So what is the will of the Father on a daily basis for us? Let's got to the source, the ultimate in all truth, the Word! First Thessalonians 5:15-19 says "See that none render evil for evil unto any man; but ever follow that which is good, both among yourselves, and to all men. Rejoice evermore. Pray without ceasing. In every thing give thanks; for this is the will of God in Christ Jesus concerning you. Quench not the Spirit."

Let me tell you a little story. A couple of years ago at summer at camp, Pastor Dennis Brannon was leading several of the services during the week. We had a great time in the Lord. At one point He was talking to me and others about our personal relationship with the Lord. This is the way that He put it to me. He said "Steve, what good will it do you if you reach 18 million meth addicts with your book and then one day you stand before the Lord and he says depart from me I never knew you?" What good will it do me to tell people about Jesus and not really have a relationship with Him? Matthew 7:21-23 says, "Not every one that saith unto me, Lord, Lord, shall enter into the kingdom of heaven; but he that doeth the will of my Father which is in heaven. Many will say to me in that day Lord, Lord, have we not prophesied in thy name? and in thy name have cast out devils? and in thy name done many wonderful works? And then will I profess unto them, I never knew you: depart from me, ye that work iniquity."

So with that in mind, first things first. This means every morning start out in prayer, being thankful, singing praises to the Lord! It's our own personal relationship that matters most to the Master! And I promise you that once you begin to develop a relationship with Him, nothing or no one can ever take His place. There is nothing that comes close, nothing that can fill the void, only He can fill the void. It's in the Word that you will find out what He is really like. Not what you or I think He is like, but what the Word of God says. You develop a relationship with the Lord, just like you would anyone else. Begin to talk to Him, read His Word, pray and be led by the Holy Spirit.

Matthew 10:16 says "Behold, I send you forth as sheep in the midst of wolves: be ye therefore wise as serpents, and harmless as doves." What I want you to know that in this world, even the Christian world there are doctrines of devils being taught. That is why it is so important to know what the Word of God says for yourself and not rely on any man to get your meat. If you are being taught anything, make sure it lines up with the Word. We have the ability to find out what the Word really says. This is a warning to not listen to every interpretation of man that you hear. Never take the attitude that you cannot be deceived, or that your church is the only right one around. It could mislead you. Always make certain that what your being taught lines up with the Word.

I must admit I have made several mistakes. But it has been through these mistakes that the Lord has shown me in the Scriptures, the deception that had been going on. This is how we learn by our mistakes. There are agents of the devil in the church. They sneak in unawares and lead people astray with false doctrine. Even though a person may seem to be the most respected person and very spiritual, they don't really care for your soul. They might seem very refined and the most wonderful man you've ever met. They are not true ministers of God.

First Timothy 4:1, 2 says, "Now the Spirit speaketh expressly, that in the latter times some shall depart from the faith, giving heed to seducing spirits, and doctrines of devils; Speaking lies in hypocrisy; having their conscience seared with a hot iron;" It is our job to be protectors of the Word of God, not only for our own lives, but also for our brothers and sisters in Christ! First Timothy 4:6 says, "If thou put the brethren in remembrance of these things, thou shalt be a good minister of Jesus Christ, nourished up in the words of faith and of good doctrine, whereunto thou hast attained." Now don't get me wrong there are many wonderful churches out there, but there are individuals that you will have to deal with, your pastor cannot always be there. Always remember that if you are spending more time in any other book than your Bible, you must make an adjustment. Make sure that no book takes up more time than your Bible.

Learning To Hate

Proverbs 8:13 says, "The fear of the Lord is to hate evil. . . ."

If there is one thing that I do know, it is that methamphetamine and its production are evil. That Satan and his demons are having a field day at you and your families expense. Hey maybe it's something else other than meth that is destroying you. Learning to hate the evil is good therapy. Let me repeat this learning to hate the evil is good therapy. I hate what it does to families. I hate the way that it kills children. I hate what it did to my mind. I hate the demons that want to destroy my family. I hate what it does to mothers and turns men and women into whores. I hate the way it makes a man whore out his wife and kids to meth. This list could go on and on. What would your list say about meth? Let's make a list of everything that you hate about meth and post it where you can see it every day. Big letters that you can see. Recently I received a letter from a man that he had wrote to crystal meth. He told meth how much he hated it. I would encourage you to write such a letter.

In order for you to begin to hate, it must come out of your mouth and be voiced to others. Especially men and women in prison. I know this can be difficult, especially when the main topic is cooking dope. Your words have power: power to rebuild and power to destroy. Teaching people to cook dope is teaching the devil's trade and doing his will for your life. There is nothing else that comes close to destroying lives like a batch of crystal meth. I know many who say and think that they control it. But you are being deceived. You are the one who is being controlled. You will never have a normal life if man-made white powders are in it.

I pray in the name of Jesus, that you will begin to hate the evil of meth and to speak out against it and it's production. The war on terrorism is a big deal. But another real war should be on the production plants overseas and here in America that produce ephedrine and pseudoephedrine. How many more children and families must be killed? Psalms chapter 97 and verse 10 says, "Ye that love the Lord, hate evil: he preserveth the souls of his saints; he delivereth them out of the hand of the wicked." The war is on, which side are you on?

Daily Accomplishments

Proverbs 13:19 says, "The desire accomplished is sweet to the soul: but it is abomination to fools to depart from evil."

Daily accomplishments are a must!

Daily accomplishments are becoming our new drug. It is a scientific fact that methamphetamine releases the dopamine in our minds, much like that of completing a task. Dopamine is released naturally. Every day what are you going? Take a good look around you. Let's start with the yard. I challenge you everyday to do something productive to your yard and house. A gallon of paint is relatively cheap. A rake doesn't cost that much. Start off with small areas and finish what you start. Start cooking dinner instead of cooking dope. Write down your goals and complete them.

Habakkuk 2:2 says, "And the Lord answered me, and said, Write the vision, and make it plain upon tables, that he may run that readeth it." Write down your visions and desires for your life and what you want to accomplish for the Lord! I encourage you men and women to become dealers again, but dealers of legal items. Sell cars, antiques, look for ways that you can better your life and supplement your income. I want to encourage you all to tithe and give to the Kingdom of God, (Read Malachi 3:6-11). Guard your family and your life.

Beware

Matthew 16:6 says, "Then Jesus said unto them, Take heed and beware of the leaven of the Pharisees and of the Sadducees."

I pray in the name of Jesus that you read this chapter carefully. In this scripture, Jesus is telling us to beware of religion. Every church has a different set of beliefs and rules and regulations that they go by.

Let me tell you what the Lord showed me. Imagine you are in a big shopping mall and all of the glass doors are closed. As you walk down the mall you are looking in and here is what you see. Each store represents a different denomination. You look in and you see a ceremonial type atmosphere, with worship of Mary going on. Next store once saved always save is being taught. Next store you can speak in tongues. The next store you can't speak in tongues. The next store there is music going on. The next store there is no music. The next store you have to be baptized in water. The next store you must be baptized in water in Jesus' name and be a member of that church. The next store they believe in the Trinity. The next store there is no Trinity. The next store there are new revelation of the Word of God being taught. The next store they have their own litera-ture other than the Bible. The next store they believe that all of the Bible isn't true. The next store they believe the Bible is all true. The next store you can get to heaven through your good works. The next store you can drink alcohol. The next store you can't drink alcohol. The next store they believe in the Holy Ghost. The next store there is no Holy Ghost. The next store they control congregation with con-demning sermons. The next store they are the only ones going to heaven. The next store they are a ministry that revolves around bash-ing other ministries. The next store they will sell you a blessing. Are starting to get what Jesus was talking about? I encourage you to guard you and your family. All I can say to all of these different stores is Know ye not what the scriptures say? Find out for yourself what the Word of God says. First Corinthians 2:2 says "For I determined not to know anything among you, save Jesus Christ, and him crucified."

Reconciliation

Second Corinthians 11:3 says, "But I fear, lest by any means as the serpent beguiled Eve through his subtility, so your minds should be corrupted from the simplicity that is in Christ."

The word simplicity, in the preceding scripture comes from the root word *Haplotes*, which means simplicity, purity, sincerity, faithfulness, and toward others helpfulness and giving assistance to others.

The Gospel of Jesus Christ is a simple message. If you keep Him at the front of your life, you will make it. That is the meaning of this book: to bring you to reconciliation with God.

Second Corinthians 5:18 says, "And all things are of God, who hath reconciled us to himself by Jesus Christ and hath given to us the ministry of reconciliation."

The word reconciliation comes from the root word *katallasso* which means a change or reconciliation from a state of enmity (enemies) between persons to one of friendship. The Lord Jesus Christ is in the reconciling business! He will set you free if you give Him a chance. Jesus has redeemed us! Jesus took upon himself our sin and became atonement. He established the relationship of peace with mankind, with God the Father.

John 5:22 says, "For the Father judgeth no man, but hath committed all judgement unto the Son."

How does God reconcile us? How would God reconcile his people that are trapped in bondage to methamphetamine? I believe that He does it through the truth. The truth is that methamphetamine and its production is sorcery, and is controlled by Satan and his demons. You can break free! Eternity is serious business—Heaven and Hell, spending eternity with God, or spending eternity separated from Him. Come to the Lord today. He loves you and wants to change your heart. He wants to restore your life and your family. If we never meet, I look forward to seeing you in heaven. God bless you and yours!

Scriptures

Section 1 Foreword

Isaiah 55:9 "For as the heavens are high than the earth, so are my ways higher than your ways, and my thoughts than your thoughts."

Isaiah 55:11 "So shall my word be that goeth forth out of my mouth: it shall not return void, but it shall accomplish that which I please, and it shall prosper in the thing whereto I sent it."

John 8:32 "You shall know the truth and the truth will set you free."

Ezekiel 37:10 "So I prophesied as he commanded me and the breath came into them and they lived, and stood up upon their feet, an exceeding great army."

Chapter 1

Job 41:6 "Shall the companions make a banquet of him? Shall they part him among the merchants?"

Revelations 18:23 "For thy merchants were the great men of the earth; for by thy sorceries were all nations deceived."

Job 41:20 "Out of his nostrils goeth smoke, as out of a seething pot or cauldron."

Job 41:33, 34 "Upon earth there is not his like, who is made without fear. He beholdeth all high things; he is a king over all the children of pride."

Isaiah 27:1 "In that day the Lord with his sore and great and strong sword shall punish leviathan the piercing serpent, even leviathan that crooked serpent; and he shall slay the dragon that is in the sea."

Revelation 20:1, 2 "And I saw an angel come down from heaven, having the key of the bottomless pit and a great chain in his hand and he laid hold on the dragon, that old serpent, which is the devil, and satan and bound him a thousand years."

Chapter 2

2 Corinthians 13:1 "This is the third time I am coming to you. IN THE MOUTH OF TWO OF THREE WITNESSES SHALL EVERY WORD BE ESTABLISHED."

Acts 13:10 "Paul with the Holy Ghost said to the sorcerer O full of all subtilty and all mischief, thou child of the devil, thou enemy of all righteousness, wilt thou not cease to pervert the right ways of the Lord!"

Chapter 3

John 10:10 "The thief cometh not, but to steal, and to kill, and to destroy: I am come that they might have life, and that they might have it more abundantly."

Psalms 103:12 "As far as the east is from the west, so far hath he removed our sins from us."

2 Corinthians 5:17 "That if any man be in Christ, he is a new creature: old things are passed away; behold all things are become new."

Matthew 4:4 "It is written, man shall not live by bread alone, but by every word that proceedeth out of the mouth of God."

Psalm 32:7 "Thou art my hiding place; thou shalt preserve me from trouble, thou shalt compass me about with songs of deliverance, selah."

James 5:16 "Confess your faults one to another, and pray one another, that ye may be healed. The effectual fervent prayer of a righteous man availeth much."

Chapter 4
2 Peter 1:16 "For we have not followed cunningly devised fables, when we made known unto you the power and coming of our Lord Jesus Christ, but were eyewitnesses of his majesty."

Chapter 5
1 Samuel 15:23 "For rebellion is as the sin of witchcraft . . ."

Ephesians 5:11 "And have no fellowship with the unfruitful works of darkness, but rather expose them."

Revelation 9:21 "Neither repented they of their murders, nor of their sorceries."

Revelation 18:23 "And the light of a candle shall shine no more at all in thee; and the voice of the bridegroom and of the bride shall be heard no more at all in thee; for thy merchants were the great men of the earth; for by thy sorceries were all nations deceived."

Revelation 21:8 "But the fearful and the unbelieving, and the abominable, and murderers, and whoremongers, and sorcerers, and idolaters, and all liars, shall have their part in the lake which burneth with fire and brimstone; which is the second death."

Revelation 22:15 "For without are dogs and sorcerers, whoremongers, murderers, idolaters, and whosever loveth and maketh a lie."

Isaiah 47:9 "But these two things shall come to thee, in a moment in one day, the loss of children, and widowhood; they shall come upon thee in their perfection for the multitude of thy sorceries and for the great abundance of thine enchantments."

Isaiah 47:12 "Stand now with thine enchantments, and with the multitudes of thy sorceries, wherein thou hast labored from thy youth; if so be thou shalt be able to profit, if so be thou mayest prevail."

Malachi 3:5 "And I will come near to you to judgement; and I will be a swift witness against the sorcerers, and against the adulterers, and against the false swearers, and against those that oppress the hireling in his wages, the widow, and the fatherless, and that turn aside the stranger from his right, and fear not me, saith the Lord of Hosts."

1 Samuel 15:23 "For rebellion is as the sin of witchcraft . . ."

Isaiah 24:16-18 "From the uttermost parts of the earth have we heard songs even glory to the righteous. But I said, My leanesss, my leaness woe unto me! the treacherous dealers have dealt treacherously; yea, the treacherous dealers have dealt very treacherously. Fear and the pit, and the snare, are upon thee, O inhabitant of the earth. And it shall come to pass, that he who fleeth from the noise of the fear shall fall into the pit; and he that cometh up out of the midst of the pit shall be taken in the snare: for the windows from on high are open, and the foundations of the earth do shake."

Acts 13:10 "O full of all subtility and all mischief, thou child of the devil, thou enemy of all righteousness, wilt thou not cease to pervert the right ways of the Lord?"

Revelation 13:16,17 "And he causeth all, both small and great, rich and poor, free and bond, to receive a mark in their right hand, or in their foreheads. And that no man might buy or sell, save he that had the mark, or the name of the beast, or the number of his name."

Revelation 14:9-11 "And the third angel followed them saying with a loud voice, If any man worship the beast and his image, and receive his mark, in his forehead, or in his hand. The same shall drink of the wine of the wrath of God, which is poured out without mixture into the cup of indignation and he shall be tormented with fire and brimstone in the presence of the holy angels, and in he presence of the Lamb. And the smoke of their torment ascendeth up forever and ever: and they have no rest day nor night, who worship the beast and his image, and whosoever receiveth the mark of his name."

Revelation 15:2 "And I saw as it were a sea of glass mingled with fire; and them that had gotten the victory over the beast, and over his image, and over his mark, and over the number of his name stand on the sea of glass, having the harps of God."

Colossians 1:12-22 "Giving thanks unto the Father, which hath made us meet to be partakers of the inheritance of the saints in light. Who hath delivered us from the power of darkness, and hath translated us into the kingdom of his dear Son. In whom we have redemption through the blood, even the forgiveness of sins. For by him were all things created, that are in heaven, and that are in earth, visible and invisible, whether they be thrones, or dominions, or principalities, or powers: all things were created by him and for him: And he is before all things and by him all things consist. And he is the head of the body, the church: who is the beginning, the first born from the dead; that in all things he might have the preeminence. And you, that were sometime alienated and enemies in your mind by wicked works, yet now hath he reconciled In the body of his flesh through death, to present you holy and unblameable and unreproveable in his sight:"

Chapter 6

Isaiah 47:9 "But these two things shall come to thee in a moment in one DAY, the LOSS OF CHILDREN, and widowhood: they shall come upon thee in their PERFECTION for the multitude of thy SORCERIES, and for the great abundance of thing ENCHANTMENTS."

2 Timothy 3:13 "But evil men and seducers shall wax worse and worse, deceiving, and being deceived."

2 Timothy 3:1-5 "This know also that in the last days perilous times shall come. For men shall be lovers of their own selves, covetous, boasters, proud, blasphemers, disobedient to parents, unthankful, unholy, without natural affection, trucebreakers, false accusers, incontinent, fierce, despisers of those that are good, traitors, heady, highminded, lovers of pleasures more than lovers of God; Having a form of godliness, but denying they power thereof: from such turn away."

2 Timothy 3:8, 9 "Now as Jannes and Jambres withstood Moses, so do these also resist the truth: men of corrupt minds, reprobate concerning the faith. But they shall proceed no further: for their folly shall be manifest unto all men, as theirs also was."

Romans 10:9 "That if thou shalt confess with thy mouth the Lord Jesus, and shalt believe in thine heart that God hath raised him from the dead, thou shalt be saved. For with the heart man believeth unrighteousness; and with the mouth confession is made unto salvation."

Chapter 8
2 Corinthians 10:3 "For though we walk in the flesh, we do not war after the flesh. (For the weapons of our warfare are not carnal, but mighty through God to the pulling down of strongholds;) Casting down imaginations and every high thing that exalteth itself against the knowledge of God, and bringing into captivity every thought to the obedience of Christ."

John 14:6 "Jesus said unto them, I am the way, the truth, and the life: no man cometh unto the Father, but by me."

John 14:2 "In my Father's house are many mansions: if it were not so, I would have told you. I go to prepare a place for you. And if I go and prepare a place for you, I will come again, and receive you unto myself; that where I am, there you may be also."

Chapter 10
<u>Matthew 18:6, 7</u> "But whoso shall offend one of these little ones which believe in me, it were better for him that a millstone were hanged about his neck, and that he were drowned in the depth of the sea. Woe unto the world because of offenses! for it must needs that offenses come; but woe to that man by whom the offenses cometh!"

Chapter 11
<u>Mark 5:26-28, 34</u> "And she had suffered many things of many physicians, and had spent all that she had, and was nothing bettered, but rather grew worse. When she had heard of Jesus, came in the press behind and touched his garment. For she said, If I may touch but his clothes, I shall be whole. And he (Jesus) said unto her, Daughter thy faith hath made thee whole: go in peace, and be whole of this plague."

<u>1 Corinthians 13:8-10</u> "Charity (pursuit of love) never faileth: but whether there be prophecies, they shall fail; whether there be tongues, they shall cease; whether there be knowledge, it shall vanish away. For we know in part and we prophesy in part. But when that which is perfect (Jesus) is come, then that which is in part shall be done away with."

Chapter 12
<u>1 Timothy 6:10</u> "For the love of money is the root of all evil: which while some coveted after, they have erred from the faith, and pierced themselves through with many sorrows."

<u>Psalm 144:1</u> "Blessed be the Lord my strength, which teacheth my hands to war and my fingers to fight!"

<u>Colossians 3:22, 23</u> "Servants, obey in all things your masters according to the flesh; not with eyeservice, as menpleasers; but in singleness of heart, fearing God: And whatsoever ye do, do it heartily, as to the Lord, and not unto men."

Chapter 13

Hebrews 4:12 "For the Word of God is quick and powerful and sharper than any two edged sword, piercing even to the dividing asunder of Soul and Spirit and of the joints and marrow and is a discerner of the thoughts and intents of the heart."

Ephesians 6:12 "For we wrestle not against flesh and blood but against principalities, against powers, against the rulers of the darkness of this world, against spiritual wickedness in high places."

Chapter 14

Luke 8:27-30 "And when he went forth (Jesus) to land, there met him out the city a certain man, which had devils long time, and ware no clothes, neither abode in any house, but in the tombs. When he saw Jesus, cried out, and fell down before him, and with a loud voice said, What have I do with thee, Jesus, thou Son of God most high? I beseech thee, torment me not. (for he had commanded the unclean to come out of the man. For often times it had caught him: and he was kept bound with chains and in fetters; and he brake the bands, and was driven into the wilderness.) And Jesus asked him, saying, What is thy name? And he said, Legion: because many devils were entered into him."

Chapter 16

Ephesians 2:1-8 "And you hath he quickened who were dead in trespasses and sins; Wherein in time past ye walked according to the course of this world, according to the prince of the power of the air, the spirit that now worketh in the children of disobedience; Among whom also we all had our conversation in times past in the lusts of our flesh, fulfilling the desires of the flesh and of the mind; and were by nature the children of wrath, even as others. But God, who is rich in mercy, for his great love wherewith he loved us, even we were dead in sins, hath quickened us together with Christ, (by grace yea re saved;) And hath raised us up together in heavenly places in Christ Jesus. That in the ages to come he might show the exceeding riches of his grace in his kindness toward us through Christ Jesus. For by grace are ye saved through faith; and that not of yourselves; it is the gift of God."

Chapter 17

<u>John 10:10</u> "The thief cometh not, but for to steal, kill and destroy:"

<u>Proverbs 27:4</u> "Wrath is cruel, and anger is outrageous; but who is able to stand before envy?"

<u>Acts 13:9, 10</u> "Then Saul, (who also is called Paul) filled with the Holy Ghost, set his eyes on him. And said, O full of all subtility and all mischief, thou child of the devil, thou enemy of all righteousness, wilt thou not cease to pervert the right ways of the Lord?"

<u>Genesis 3:1</u> "Now the serpent was more subtle than any beast of the field which the Lord God had made."

<u>Matthew 25:41</u> "Then shall he say also unto them on the left hand, Depart from me, ye cursed, into everlasting fire, prepared for the devil and his angels."

<u>Romans 12:21</u> "Be not overcome of evil, but overcome evil with good."

Chapter 18

<u>Job 18:10-15, 21</u> "The snare is laid for him in the ground, and a trap for him in the way Terrors shall make him afraid on every side, and shall drive him to his feet. His strength shall be hunger-bitten and destruction shall be ready at his side. It shall devour the strength of his kin: even the first born of death shall devour his strength. His confidence shall be rooted out of his tabernacle, (house), and it shall bring him to the king of terrors. It shall dwell in his tabernacle because it is none of his: brimstone shall be scattered upon his habitation. Surely such are the dwellings of the wicked, and this is the

place of him that knoweth not God."

Ezekiel 28:14-16 "Thou art the anointed cherub that covereth and I have set thee so: thou wast upon the holy mountain of God; thou hast walked up and down in the midst of the stones of fire. Thou was perfect in thy ways from the day that thou wast created, till iniquity was found in thee. By the multitude of thy merchandise they have filled the midst of thee with violence, and thou hast sinned: therefore I will cast thee as profane out of the mountain of God: and I will cast thee to the ground, I will lay thee before kings, that they may behold thee."

Isaiah 14:13-16 "For thou hast said in thin heart, I (Lucifer) will ascend into heaven, I will exalt my throne above the stars of God: I will sit also upon the mount of the congregation, in the sides of the north: I will ascend above the heights of the clouds; I will be like the most High. Yet thou shalt be brought down to hell, to the sides of the pit. They that see thee shall narrowly look upon thee and consider thee saying, Is this the man that made the earth to tremble, that did shake the kingdoms:"

Revelations 20:1-3 "And I saw an angel come down from heaven, having the key of the bottomless pit and a great chain in his hand. And he laid hold on the dragon, that old serpent, which is the Devil and satan and bound him a thousand years. Cast him into the bottomless pit and shut him up and set a seal upon him, that he should deceive the nations no more, till the thousand years should be fulfilled and after that he must be loosed for a little season."

Section 2 Chapter 1
Psalm 144:1 "BLESSED be the Lord my strength, which teacheth my hands to war and my fingers to fight;"

Matthew 16:26 "For what is a man profited, if he shall gain the whole world, and lose his own soul? of what shall a man give in exchange for his soul?"

Hebrews 11:6 "But without faith it is impossible to please him: for he that cometh to God must believe that he is and that he is a rewarder of them that diligently seek him."

Chapter 2
Psalm 106:36-39 "And they served their idols (methamphetamine) which were a snare onto them. Yea, they sacrificed their sons and their daughters onto devils. And shed innocent blood, even the blood of their daughters, whom they sacrificed onto the idols of Canaan: and the land was polluted with blood. Thus were they defiled with their own works and went a whoring with their own inventions."

Chapter 3
1 John 2:27 "But the anointing which ye have received of him abideth in you, and ye need not that any man teach you: but as the same anointing teacheth you of all things and is truth and is no lie, and even as it hath taught you, ye shall abide in him."

Romans 10:17 "So then faith cometh by hearing and hearing by the word of God."

Hebrews 11:1 "Now faith is the substance of things hoped for, the evidence of things not seen."

James 1:3, 4 "Knowing this, that the trying of your faith worketh patience. Patience is a great lesson to learn and one that must be learned by someone that is overcoming a meth addiction. But let patience have her perfect work, that ye may be perfect and entire, wanting nothing."

Hebrews 11:6 "But without faith it is impossible to please him: for he that cometh to God must believe that he is, and that he is a rewarder of them that diligently seek him."

John 8:31 "Then said Jesus to those Jews which believed on him, If ye continue in my word, then are ye my disciples indeed."

Chapter 4

Luke 18:27 "And he said The things which are impossible with men are possible with God." Luke 1:37 says, "For with God nothing shall be impossible."

Hebrews 13:8 "Jesus Christ the same yesterday, and today and forever."

Job 5:8-11 "I would seek onto God and unto God would I commit my cause: Which doeth great things and unsearchable; marvellous things without number. Who giveth rain upon the earth and sendeth waters upon the fields: To set up on high those that be low; that those which mourn may be exalted to safety."

Job 5:12 "He disappointeth the devices of the crafty, so that their hands cannot perform their enterprise."

Job 5:13, 14 "He taketh the wise in their own craftiness; and the counsel of the froward is carried headlong. What will begin to happen to them, saying they meet with darkness in the daytime, and grope in the noonday as in the night."

John 8:12 "Then spake Jesus again unto them saying, I am the light of the world, he that followeth me shall not walk in darkness, but shall have the light of life."

Acts 13:12 "Then the deputy, when he saw what was done, believed, being astonished at the doctrine of the Lord."

Chapter 6

<u>Acts 5:14</u> "And believers were the more added to the Lord, multitudes both of men and women."

<u>Luke 10:2</u> "Therefore said he unto them, the harvest truly is great, but the labourers are few: pray ye therefore the Lord of the harvest, that he would send forth labourers into his harvest."

<u>James 2:17-20</u> "Even so faith, if it hath not works is dead, being alone. yea a man may say, Thou hast faith, and I have works: shew me thy faith without thy works and I will shew thee my faith by my works. Thou believest that there is one God; thou doest well: the devils also believe and tremble. But wilt thou know, O vain man, that faith without works is dead?"

<u>John 8:31, 32</u> "Then said Jesus to those Jews which believed on him, If ye continue in my word, then are ye my disciples indeed; And ye shall know the truth and the truth shall make you free."

Chapter 7

<u>Matthew 10:1</u> "And when he had called unto him his twelve disciples, he gave them power against unclean spirits, to cast them out, and to heal all manner of sickness and all manner of disease"

<u>Mark 6:7</u> "And he called unto him the twelve, and began to send them forth by two and two; and gave the power over unclean spirits"

<u>Luke 9:1, 2</u> "Then he called his twelve disciples together, and gave them power and authority over all devils, and to cure diseases. And he sent them to preach the Kingdom of God, and to heal the sick"

<u>Luke 10:1</u> "After these things the Lord appointed other seventy also, and sent them two and two before his face into every city and place, whither he himself would come"

<u>Luke 10:17</u> "And the seventy returned again with joy, saying, Lord even the devils are subject unto us through thy name"

<u>John 8:31</u> ". . . If ye continue in my word, then are ye my disciples indeed;"

<u>Mark 16:17</u> "And these signs shall follow them that believe; In my name shall they cast out devils;"

Chapter 8

<u>Mark 9:18</u> "And wheresoever he taketh him, he teareth him; and he foameth, and gnasheth with him teeth, and pineth away: and I spake to thy disciples that they should cast him out; and they could not."

<u>Mark 9:22</u> "And often times it hath cast him into the fire, and into the waters, to destroy him: but if thou canst do anything, have compassion on us, and help us."

<u>Mark 9:23</u> "Jesus said unto him, If thou canst believe, all things are possible to him that believeth"

<u>Mark 9:29</u> "This kind can come forth by nothing but by prayer and fasting."

<u>Luke 11:20</u> "But if I with the finger of God cast out devils, no doubt the kingdom of God is come upon you."

Chapter 9

<u>1 John 2:27</u> "But the anointing which ye have received of him abideth in you, and ye need not that any man teach you: but as the same anointing teacheth you of all things, and is truth, and is no lie, and even as it hath taught you, ye shall abide in him"

<u>Matthew 12:43, 44</u> "When the unclean spirit is gone out of a man, he walketh through dry places, seeking rest, and findeth none. Then he

saith, I will return into my house from whence I came out; and when he is come, he findeth it empty, swept and garnished."

Chapter 11
<u>Matthew 12:31</u> "Wherefore I say unto you, All manner of sin and blasphemy shall be forgiven unto men: but the blasphemy against the Holy Ghost shall not be forgiven unto men. And Whosoever speaketh a word against the Son of man, it shall be forgiven him: but whosoever speaketh against the Holy Ghost, it shall not be forgiven him, neither in this world, neither in the world to come."

<u>Philippians 3:18</u> "For many walk, of whom I have told you often, and now tell you even weeping, that they are the enemies of the cross of Christ."

Chapter 12
<u>1 Corinthians 16:15</u> "I beseech you, brethren, (ye know the house of Stephanas, that it is the first fruits of Achaia, and that they have addicted themselves to the ministry of the saints,)"

<u>Hebrew 6:12</u> "That ye be not slothful, but followers of them who through faith and patience inherit the promises."

Chapter 13
<u>1 Thessalonians 5:15-19</u> "See that none render evil for evil unto any man; but ever follow that which is good, both among yourselves, and to all men. Rejoice evermore. Pray without ceasing. In every thing give thanks; for this is the will of God in Christ Jesus concerning you. Quench not the Spirit."

<u>Matthew 7:21-23</u> "Not every one that saith unto me, Lord, Lord, shall enter into the kingdom of heaven; but he that doeth the will of my Father which is in heaven. Many will say to me in that day Lord, Lord, have we not prophesied in thy name? and in thy name have cast out devils? and in thy name done many wonderful works? And

then will I profess unto them, I never knew you: depart from me, ye that work iniquity."

Matthew 10:16 "Behold, I send you forth as sheep in the midst of wolves: be ye therefore wise as serpents, and harmless as doves."

1 Timothy 4:1, 2 "Now the Spirit speaketh expressly, that in the latter times some shall depart from the faith, giving heed to seducing spirits, and doctrines of devils; Speaking lies in hypocrisy; having their conscience seared with a hot iron;"

1 Timothy 4:6 "If thou put the brethren in remembrance of these things, thou shalt be a good minister of Jesus Christ, nourished up in the words of faith and of good doctrine, whereunto thou hast attained."

Chapter 14
Proverbs 8:13 "The fear of the Lord is to hate evil. . . ."

Psalms 97:10 "Ye that love the Lord, hate evil: he preserveth the souls of his saints; he delivereth them out of the hand of the wicked."

Chapter 15
Proverbs 13:19 "The desire accomplished is sweet to the soul: but it is abomination to fools to depart from evil."

Habakkuk 2:2 "And the Lord answered me, and said, Write the vision, and make it plain upon tables, that he may run that readeth it."

Chapter 16
Matthew 16:6 "Then Jesus said unto them, Take heed and beware of the leaven of the Pharisees and of the Sadducees."

1 Corinthians 2:2 "For I determined not to know anything among you, save Jesus Christ, and him crucified."

Chapter 17

<u>2 Corinthians 11:3</u> "But I fear, lest by any means as the serpent beguiled Eve through his subtility, so your minds should be corrupted from the simplicity that is in Christ."

<u>2 Corinthians 5:18</u> "And all things are of God, who hath reconciled us to himself by Jesus Christ and hath given to us the ministry of reconciliation."

<u>John 5:22</u> "For the Father judgeth no man, but hath committed all judgement unto the son."

STEPS TO SALVATION

1. We have all separated ourselves from God. *Romans 3:23* "For all have sinned and fall short of the glory of God."
2. But He still loves us. . . *John 3:16* "For God so loved the world that he gave His one and only begotten Son, that whosoever believes in Him shall not perish but have eternal life."
3. So He has made a way for us to know Him! *Romans 5:8* "God demonstrates His own love for us in this: While we were yet sinners Christ died for us."
4. All we have to do is believe. *Romans 10:9* "If you confess with your mouth, Jesus is Lord, and believe in your heart that God raised Him from the dead, you will be saved."
5. And receive His gift! *Romans 3:24* "(all) are justified freely by His grace through the redemption that came by Christ Jesus."

PRAYER OF SALVATION

Heavenly Father I come to you as a sinner. I acknowledge that I am in need of a Savior. I believe that Jesus is the Son of God. I believe that He died on the cross for me and my sins. I believe that He was raised from the dead and is seated at Your right hand. Jesus, I ask You to come into my heart and be the Lord and Savior of my life. I ask You to forgive me of my sins, cleanse me and make me whole in Jesus Name. Thank you Lord for saving me now.

Steve Box Ministries
P.O. Box 122
Pierce City, MO 65723
417-476-3106
Fax: 417-476-5872
Email: steve@methequalssorcery.com
Web page: www.methequalssorcery.com